Common Ground
Between
Islam and Buddhism

Common Ground
Between
Islam and Buddhism

By Reza Shah-Kazemi

With an essay by Shaykh Hamza Yusuf

Introduced by
H. H. the Fourteenth Dalai Lama
H. R. H. Prince Ghazi bin Muhammad
Professor Mohammad Hashim Kamali

FONS VITAE

First published in 2010 by
Fons Vitae
49 Mockingbird Valley Drive
Louisville, KY 40207
http://www.fonsvitae.com
Email: fonsvitaeky@aol.com

Library of Congress Control Number: 2010925171
ISBN 978–1891785627

With gratitude to the Thesaurus Islamicus Foundation
for the use of the fourteenth century Qur'ānic *shamsiyya*
lotus image found in *Splendours of Qur'ān Calligraphy
and Illumination* by Martin Lings. We also thank Justin
Majzub for his artistic rendition of this beautiful motif.

Printed in Canada

Contents

Contents, continued

THE DALAI LAMA

FOREWORD

This is an important and pioneering book, which seeks to find common ground between the teachings of Islam and of Buddhism. It is my hope that on the basis of this common ground, followers of each tradition may come to appreciate the spiritual truths their different paths entail and from this develop a basis for respect for each others' practice and beliefs. This may not have occurred very often before, because there has been so little opportunity for real understanding between these two great traditions. This book attempts to set that right.

The Buddha taught that every sentient being has a mind or consciousness whose fundamental nature is essentially pure, unpolluted by mental distortions. We refer to that nature as Buddha nature or the seed of enlightenment. From that point of view every being can eventually achieve perfection. And also, because the nature of the mind is pure, we believe that all negative aspects can ultimately be removed from it. When our mental attitude is positive, the negative actions of body and speech automatically cease. Because we believe every sentient being has such potential, all are equal; everyone has the right to be happy and to overcome suffering. The whole Buddhist way of life is based upon principles of deep respect for the welfare of all our fellow beings. It is a system based on the practice of compassion.

My Muslim friends have explained to me that since God is characterised as compassionate and merciful, faithful Muslims are actually offering complete submission to the ideal of universal compassion. By this means God's compassion can flow through the actions of the faithful. Such a practice is clearly a way of purifying the mind and seems to parallel what the Buddha himself said about the importance of actually living your life in a compassionate, ethical way. Thus, from a Buddhist point of view, the practice of Islam is evidently a spiritual path of salvation.

Clearly, compassion lies at the heart of the teachings of both Islam and Buddhism, as it also lies at the heart of other great religious traditions. It is my heartfelt hope that recognition of this fundamental shared principle will be grounds for Muslims and Buddhists to overcome any sense of wariness they may feel about each other and develop a fruitful, trusting friendship. The time has certainly come for followers of the world's great religions to work together to create a more compassionate and peaceful world.

I would like to express my deep gratitude to my friend Prince Ghazi bin Muhammad who has several times welcomed me to Jordan and who as a result of our conversations then has initiated this admirable project. Conversations with him and other Muslim friends confirm me in my conviction of the profound value of encouraging dialogue between the world's great spiritual traditions. I pray that its consequences may be fruitful and far-reaching.

January 21, 2010

In the Name of God, the Compassionate, the Merciful
May Peace and Blessings be upon the Prophet Muhammad

Introduction to *Common Ground*
By H. R. H. Prince Ghazi bin Muhammad

The Religions of the World and World Peace

As of the year 2010 CE, 1431 AH, at least 80% of the world's population of 6.7 billion humans belong to four of the world's many religions. Four out of five people on earth are either Christian (32%), Muslim (23%), Hindu (14%) or Buddhist (12%). Since religion (from the Latin '*re-ligio*', meaning to 're-tie' [man to Heaven]) is arguably the most powerful force in shaping people's attitudes and behaviour — in theory if not in practice — it follows logically that if there is to be peace and harmony in the world there must peace and harmony between religions as such, and in particular between the world's four largest religions.

On October 13th 2007, 138 of the world's leading Muslim scholars and intellectuals (including such figures as the Grand Muftis of Egypt, Syria, Jordan, Oman, Bosnia, Russia, and Istanbul) sent an Open Letter to the religious leaders of Christianity. It was addressed to the leaders of the Christian churches and denominations of the entire world, starting with His Holiness Pope Benedict XVI. In essence, the Open Letter proposed, based on verses from the Holy Qur'ān and the Holy Bible, that Islam and Christianity share, at their core, the twin 'golden' commandments of the paramount importance of loving God and loving one's neighbour. Based on this joint common ground, it called for peace and harmony between Christians and Muslims worldwide.

That Open Letter led to a historical global peace movement between Muslims and Christians specifically (as can be seen on www.acommonword.com), and whilst it has not reduced wars as such between Muslims and Christians or ended mutual hatred and prejudice, it has done a lot of good, by the Grace of God, and has noticeably changed the tone between Muslim and Christian religious leaders and somewhat deepened true understanding of each other's religions in significant ways. The *A Common Word* initiative was certainly not alone on the world's stage in attempting to make things better between people of faith (one thinks in particular of the *Alliance of Civilization*s, H. M. King Abdullah of Saudi Arabia's Interfaith Initiative and President

Obama's Cairo 2009 speech), but we think it nevertheless significant that, for example, according to the October 2009 Pew Global Report the percentage of Americans harbouring negative opinions about Islam was 53% when only a few years earlier it was 59%. It is thus possible to ameliorate tensions between two religious communities (even though conflicts and wars rage and indeed have increased in number over that same period of time) when religious leaders and intellectuals reach out to each other with the right religious message.

It was with all these things in mind that, after detailed discussions with H.H. the 14th Dalai Lama, we conceived of the present initiative. We commissioned one of the Royal Academy's Fellows, Dr. Reza Shah-Kazemi — a respected specialist in Islamic mysticism and a leading author in comparative religion — to write an essay on the topic, which we then asked him to expand into this treatise. We hope and pray that this book will be blessed with the same kind of global effect between Muslims and Buddhists that *A Common Word Between Us and You* did between Muslims and Christians.

Why Do We Need '*Common Ground*'?

The specific intention and goal of the commission was to identify a spiritual 'Common Ground' (authentically based on the religious sacred texts of Islam and Buddhism) between Muslims and Buddhists that will enable both communities to love and respect each other not merely as human beings in general, but also *as Muslims and Buddhists in particular*. In other words, we hoped to find out and understand what in our two great religions — despite all of the many irreconcilable and unbridgeable doctrinal, theological, juridical and other differences that we do have between us and that we cannot and must not deny — we have in common that will enable us to practise more loving mercy and respect towards each other more *because* we are Muslims and Buddhists, and not simply because we are all human beings. We believe that, despite the dangers of syncretism, finding religious Common Ground is fruitful, because Muslims at least will never be able to be whole-heartedly enthusiastic about any ethic that does not even mention God or refer back to Him. For God says in the Holy Qur'ān:

> *But he who turneth away from remembrance of Me, his will be a narrow life, and I shall bring him blind to the assembly on the Day of Resurrection.* (The Holy Qur'ān, *Ta Ha*, 20:124)

And also:

> *Restrain thyself along with those who cry unto their Lord at morn and evening, seeking His Countenance; and let not thine eyes overlook them, desiring the pomp of the life of the world; and obey not him whose heart We have made heedless of Our remembrance, who followeth his own lust and whose case hath been abandoned.* (The Holy Qur'ān, *Al-Kahf,* 18:28)

This explains why we do not simply propose a version of the Second 'Golden' Commandment ('Love thy Neighbour') — versions of which are indeed to be found in the same texts of Islam and Buddhism (just as they are to be found in the sacred texts of Judaism, Christianity, Hinduism, Confucianism and Taoism amongst other religions): without the First 'Golden' Commandment ('Love thy God'), the Second Commandment on its own inherently risks being spiritually devoid of truth, and thus risks descending into a superficial sentimentalism without true virtue and goodness; it risks being a secular ethic taking its stance on moods which we can conjure up to ourselves on occasion, requiring nothing from the soul, risking nothing, changing nothing, deceiving all.

On the other hand, one of the greatest ironies of many religious practitioners is that despite the fact that their religions call for mercy and respect between people, they disparage others (and deny them that mercy and respect) if those others do not undertake the same paths of loving mercy as them. Thus love of their own religions makes them *less* lovingly merciful to other people rather making them *more* merciful to other people! This seems to me as a Muslim to be particularly ironic, because in all four traditional *Sunni* Juridical Schools of Thought (*Madhahib*), as well as in traditional *Shi'a* thought and *Ibadhi* thought — that is to say, in all the traditional juridical schools of thought in Islam as such) — a person's choice of religion is *not* grounds for hostility against them (if they are not first hostile to Muslims). Rather, Muslims are required to behave with mercy and justice to all, believers and non-believers alike. God says in the Holy Qur'ān:

> *Tell those who believe to forgive those who hope not for the days of God; in order that He may requite folk what they used to earn. / Whoso doeth right, it is for his soul, and whoso doeth wrong, it is against it. And afterward unto*

your Lord ye will be brought back. (The Holy Qur'ān, *Al-Jathiyah*, 45:14–15)

The same is clear in the following passage from the Holy Qur'ān which starts by citing a prayer of earlier believers:

'Our Lord! Make us not a trial for those who disbelieve, and forgive us, our Lord! Lo! Thou, only Thou, are the Mighty, the Wise'. / Verily ye have in them a goodly pattern for everyone who looketh to God and the Last Day. And whosoever may turn away, lo! still God, He is the Absolute, the Owner of Praise. / It may be that God will ordain love between you and those of them with whom ye are at enmity. God is Mighty, and God is Forgiving, Merciful. / God forbiddeth you not those who warred not against you on account of religion and drove you not out from your homes, that ye should show them kindness and deal justly with them. Lo! God loveth the just dealers. (The Holy Qur'ān, *Al-Mumtahinah*, 60:5–8)

Thus Muslims must on principle show loving mercy and respect to all those who are not waging war on them or driving them from their homes (these thus being the conditions for just, defensive war in Islam). Muslims must not make their mercy conditional upon other people's mercy, but it is nevertheless psychologically almost inevitable that people will better appreciate their fellows more when they know their fellows are also trying to show mercy and respect to all. At least that was one of our chief assumptions in commissioning this book.

The *Common Ground*

Turning to the book itself, we think it not amiss to say that it has proved to be, by the grace of God, in general a stunning piece of scholarship and a display of depth of understanding and grandness of soul on behalf of the author. That is not to say that every Muslim — or every Buddhist — will accept, or even understand, everything that the author says, but nevertheless it can fairly be said that the book is generally normative from the Islamic point of view (especially in that it is deliberately based on the Holy Qur'ān, the *Hadith* and the insights of the great scholar and mystic Abu Hamid Al-Ghazali) and that it examines all the major schools of Buddhist thought (as I understand them). Moreover, the book shows beyond any reasonable doubt some very important similarities and parallels between Islam and Buddhism, and in particular the following:

(1) The belief in the Ultimate Truth (*Al-Haqq*) who is also Absolutely One, and who is Absolute Reality, and the Source of Grace and Guidance to human beings.

(2) The belief that each soul is accountable to a principle of justice in the Hereafter, and that this principle is rooted in the very nature of Absolute Reality.

(3) The belief in the categorical moral imperative of exercising compassion and mercy to all, if not in the central cosmogonic and eschatological functions of mercy (by this we mean the idea that the world was created through Mercy, and that through Mercy we are saved and delivered).

(4) The belief that human beings are capable of supra-rational knowledge, the source both of salvation in the Hereafter and enlightenment in the here-below.

(5) The belief in the possibility of a sanctified state for human beings, and the conviction that all should aspire to this state of sanctity.

(6) The belief in the efficacy and necessity of spiritual *practice*: whether this take the form of fervent prayer, contemplative meditation, or methodic invocation.

(7) The belief in the necessity of detachment from the world, from the ego and its passional desires.

As regards the Buddha's not mentioning of God as Creator, this is definitely an absolute difference between Muslims and Buddhists but if it is understood that the One is God, and that the Buddha's silence on the One as Creator is not a denial as such, then it is possible to say that the points above certainly make for substantial 'Common Ground' between Islam and Buddhism, despite the many unbridgeable differences between them. Certainly, these points can be taken as constituting or '*establishing*' the core of religion — and not being '*divided*' therein, and this is precisely what God says in the Holy Qur'ān is the essential message of the most important messengers of God:

> *He hath ordained for you that religion which He commended unto Noah, and that which We inspire in thee (Muhammad), and that which We commended unto Abraham and Moses and Jesus, saying: Establish the religion, and be not divided therein. Dreadful for the idolaters is that unto which*

thou callest them. God chooseth for Himself whom He will,
and guideth unto Himself him who turneth (toward Him).
(The Holy Qur'ān, *Al-Shura*, 42:13)

One might also say that these points also make up the substance of
the Two Greatest Commandments: the belief in the One Absolute
Truth and striving for detachment from the world, the ego and the
body through spiritual practices and striving for sanctity (and hence
supra-rational knowledge) might be considered an inverse way of
achieving the First Commandment, and the categorical imperative
of compassion and mercy is clearly the Second Commandment in
different words, if not the First Commandment as well (with the immortality of the soul being indicated in both Commandments by the
naming of the whole *'heart'*). And God knows best.

People of the Scripture (*Ahl Al-Kitab*)

All of the above leads us to conclude as Muslims that the Buddha,
whose basic guidance one in ten people on earth have been in
principle following for the last 2500 years, was, in all likelihood
— and God knows best — one of God's great Messengers, even if
many Muslims will not accept everything in the Pali Canon as being
authentically attributable to the Buddha. For if the Buddha is not
mentioned in the Holy Qur'ān by name, nevertheless it is clear that
God says that every people had their own *'warner'* and that there
were Messengers not mentioned in the Holy Qur'ān:

Lo! We have sent thee with the Truth, a bearer of glad tidings
and a warner; and there is not a nation but a warner hath
passed among them. (The Holy Qur'ān, *Al-Fatir*, 35:24)

Verily We sent messengers before thee, among them those
of whom We have told thee, and some of whom We have
not told thee; and it was not given to any messenger that he
should bring a portent save by God's leave, but when God's
commandment cometh (the cause) is judged aright, and the
followers of vanity will then be lost. (The Holy Qur'ān, *Al-*
Ghafir, 40:78)

It seems to us then that the Umayyads and the Abbasids were entirely correct in regarding Buddhists as if they were 'Ahl Al-Kitab'
(*'Fellow People of a Revealed Scripture'*). This is in fact how mil-
lions of ordinary Muslim believers have unspokenly regarded their

pious Buddhists neighbours for hundreds of years, despite what their scholars will tell them about doctrinal difference between the two faiths.

On a more personal note, may I say that I had read Zen Buddhist texts as a younger man when studying in the West (such as some of the writings of D.T. Suzuki and such as Eugen Herrigel's seminal *Zen in the Art of Archery*). I had greatly appreciated them, without for all that being fully able to situate Buddhism in the context of my own faith, Islam. More recently, I had noticed in myself an effect when meeting with H. H. the Dalai Lama. It was simply this: I performed the five daily prayers with greater concentration, and during the rest of the day I was better able to monitor my own thoughts, and censor and control my own impulses more easily. I did not have any particular urge to go out and learn more about Buddhism, as one might expect, but I nevertheless realised that there was something positive taking place. I asked my friend Shaykh Hamza Yusuf Hanson (who I knew had read a lot about Buddhism) why he thought this happened, and he wisely answered that this was because: 'Buddhists are heirs to a very powerful spiritual training'. Thus I am personally very gratified to learn of the underlying Common Ground between Islam and Buddhism in an explicit manner. Indeed, as a Muslim I am relieved and delighted — if I may say so — to know that one eighth of the world who is not Muslim practises Buddhism and makes the practice of compassion and mercy the centre of their lives (in theory at least). And I hope that this book will lead to Muslims and Buddhists vying in the compassion and mercy which is at the core of both their religions. God says in the Holy Qur'ān:

> *And unto thee have We revealed the Scripture with the truth, confirming whatever Scripture was before it, and a watcher over it. So judge between them by that which God hath revealed, and follow not their desires away from the truth which hath come unto thee. For each We have appointed a law and a way. Had God willed He could have made you one community. But that He may try you by that which He hath given you (He hath made you as ye are). So vie one with another in good works. Unto God ye will all return, and He will then inform you of that wherein ye differ.* (The Holy Qur'ān, *Al-Ma'idah*, 5:48)

Earlier *Common Ground*?

It would be amiss not to mention that although this book may represent one of the first — if not the first — major attempt at a scholarly spiritual comparison between Buddhism as such and Islam as such in our modern age, there have been some very brilliant and serious intellectual and spiritual exchanges in the past between Islam and the 'Three (Great) Teachings' of China (Confucianism, Taoism and Buddhism). This is evinced in particular by the works of indigenous Chinese Muslims (the '*Han Kitab*') during the sixteenth, seventeenth and eighteenth centuries, and in particular the two figures *Wang Daiyu* (ca. 1570–1660 CE) and *Liu Zhi* (ca. 1670–1724 CE). This work has been recently brought to light and translated into English (ironically, it is more or less unknown in Arabic and in modern Chinese) by Professors William Chittick, Sachiko Murata and Tu Weiming. Currently this team of scholars has produced the two following seminal books: (1) *Chinese Gleams of Sufi Light: Wang Tai-yü's 'Great Learning of the Pure and Real' and Liu Chih's 'Displaying the Concealment of the Real Realm'* (State University of New York Press, 2000); (2) *The Sage Learning of Liu Zhi: Islamic Thought in Confucian Terms* (Cambridge, MA, Harvard University Asia Centre, 2009). They are also working on Wang Daiyu's *The Real Commentary on the True Teaching* (first published in 1642 CE). These works represent a critical resource for mutual understanding between China and Islam, and scholars interested in delving further into spiritual comparisons between Islam and Buddhism (as well as Confucianism and Taoism) could not do better than to start here. We hope that these treasures will be translated into Arabic and modern Chinese and made widely available. When we make full use of the wisdom of the past, and combine it with the knowledge of today, we are better equipped to face the uncertainties of the future.

And all praise be to God, the Lord of the worlds.

The opinions expressed above represent solely Prince Ghazi's personal and private views and do not represent the views of the government and people of Jordan in any way; nor are they meant to bear upon political issues in any form whatsoever.

H. R. H. Prince Ghazi bin Muhammad
March 2010

Preface
by Professor Mohammad Hashim Kamali

The *Common Word* initiative of one hundred and thirty-eight Muslim religious leaders and academics, which advanced Muslim-Christian dialogue along theological grounds and themes of common concern to both religions, has borne fruit thanks to the earnest subsequent efforts and organizational support of numerous distinguished personalities on both sides. The Royal Aal Bayt Foundation for Islamic Thought in Jordan took the initiative in September 2007 to formulate a Muslim response to Pope Benedict XVI's somewhat controversial Regensberg lecture of the previous year. In the meantime, follow-up encounters took place between the Pope and Muslim leaders. Instead of engaging with the Pope from a defensive posture, the Muslim leaders launched the Common Word initiative reflecting the Qur'ānic invocation asking Muslims to call on the followers of scripture to *come to a word common between us and you...* (3:64) as a focus of their dialogue. The positive response from the Christian side led to several encounters and international conferences which opened new vistas of beneficial dialogue with their Muslim counterparts.

Muslim leaders are now proposing a second chapter to *A Common Word*, this time between Islam and Buddhism: *Common Ground*. The present book advances a seminal discourse exploring Islam's commonalities with the teachings of the Buddha. Like its antecedent, which found common scriptural grounds between the Bible and the Qur'ān, the present attempt underscores spiritual and moral affinities between the Qur'ān, the Pali Canon, the Mahayana scriptures and other Buddhist texts.

This book does not shy away from acknowledging the existence of many fundamental differences, even unbridgeable gaps, separating Islam and Buddhism — starting with the leading question, whether Buddhism can be called a theistic religion, or even a religion at all. Answers to such questions are given, and the author advances an equally persuasive discourse on significant spiritual and moral commonalities between Islam and Buddhism. It is an attempt at understanding some of the central principles of Buddhism in the light of Islamic spirituality that uncovers considerable common ground between them. Buddhism is more of a network of spiritual schools of thought than a unified religion, yet all Buddhist schools are united on the fundamental teachings of Buddha as expressed in the *Pali Canon* and manifested especially in its two leading schools, the Theravada and the Mahayana.

Common Ground begins by drawing a distinction between the doctrinal creed (*'aqīda*) of Islam and its spiritual wisdom (*ma'rifa*) which relates more closely to contemplation, purification of the heart, and the mystical dimensions which both religious traditions tend towards. Even at the level of *'aqīda*, although Buddhism is clearly non-theistic, the ultimate Reality affirmed by Buddhist thought, and the supreme goal sought by it, corresponds closely with the Essence (*al-Dhāt*) of God in Islam. Buddhism cultivates consciousness of the Absolute, and the quest for its realization through ethical teaching and praxis. The transcendental journey and quest toward the Absolute also shares common ground with what is known in Islam as *dhikr Allāh* (remembrance of God). *Dharma*, a major principle of Buddhism, comprises several meanings, including teaching, norm, law, truth and reality. It is the nearest equivalent of *al-Haqq* in Islam, which similarly comprises a number of parallel meanings. Suffering (*dukkha*), another theme of Buddhism, emanates from an innate thirst (*tanhā*) of one's untamed and unbridled ego for the perishable things of this world. One must overcome thirst for the ephemeral both for the sake of one's own relief from suffering and for the sake of liberating others from it. The opposite of suffering is not only a state of ease but that of the highest good, or *Nirvāna*—the Absolute which transcends the ego in all its states. *Karunā* (loving compassion), in the sense of participation in the suffering of others, is a near equivalent of *Rahmah* in Islam, both of which are expressive, on the human plane, of a principle which is rooted in the consciousness of the Absolute. This thought provoking study of Buddhist teachings also finds parallels between *Shūnya* (the Void) and the first *Shahāda* ('no god but God'), especially in their negation of false deities; between *Anicca* (impermanence) and *Zuhd* (detachment from the material world); between *Tanhā* (desire, thirst) and *hawā* (capricious desire); and between *anattā* (no soul) and *fanā'* (extinction of the self). Only the *Dharma*, *Nirvāna*, and *Shūnya*—what would be called the essence of God, beyond all conceivable qualities, in Islamic terms—is absolute, eternal and infinite; all else is transient, and thirst for the transient is the seed of all suffering. Mahayana Buddhism, which is seen by many as coming close in some respects to belief in a 'Personal God' with diverse traits, without whose grace and mercy one cannot attain salvation, comes close on a metaphysical plane to the Islamic conception of divinity. The practice of the *Nembutsu* (veneration of the celestial Buddha) is predicated on the power of the absolute Other, or *Tariki* (surrender of one's self-will to the Eternal other), which strikingly resembles the Islamic doctrine of *Tawakkul* (reliance and trust in God).

Analogous rather than identical as these concepts may be, this effort to find common ground in the essence of spirituality and devotion between Islam and Buddhism is a substantial one, and could well present a keenly persuasive basis of harmony between their adherents.

The book also develops fresh insights into the teachings of the Qur'ān and Sunna, suggesting that Buddhists may from the Islamic viewpoint be regarded as followers of a revealed scripture and thus considered as *Ahl al-Kitāb*. A theological recognition of this kind is likely to enable the adherents of both religions to appreciate and mutually respect the religious teachings of the other. An earnest attempt is thus made to help Muslims to see Buddhism as a true religion or *Dīn*, and Buddhists to see Islam as an authentic *Dharma*.

Muslim schools and jurists have differed on the understanding of the Qur'ānic designation *Ahl al-Kitāb*. Whereas many have confined the term to only the Jews and Christians, the Hanafī and Shāfiʻī schools maintain it comprises all who have followed a prophet and a revealed scripture, which would include those who believed in the psalms of David, and the scrolls (*suhuf*) of Abraham. Many have extended this status to Zoroastrians and Sabaeans. Imam al-Shāfiʻī (d. 820 CE) is critical of those who denied the status of *Ahl al-Kitāb* to Zoroastrians on the authority of an unequivocal ruling of caliph ʻAlī b. Abī Tālib (d. 661 CE) in their favour.

The proponents of this open interpretation of *Ahl al-Kitāb* have relied on the Qur'ānic verse (87:19), which refers as sources of guidance to the *earliest books* (*al-suhuf al-ūlā*), *the Books of Abraham and Moses*; and then also (Q.26:196), which refers to *the Books of earlier peoples* (*zubur al-awwalīn*), that concurred with much of the Qur'ānic guidance. The word *zubur* (scriptures) also occurs in (Q.35:25) immediately following a reference to the apostles of old that came with *clear signs and Scriptures* (*bi'l-bayyināt wa bi'z-zubur*). Three other references to *zubur* in the Qur'ān (3:184; 16:44; 54:52) also sustain the understanding that *zubur* were Scriptures of lesser magnitude compared to the Torah, Bible, and Qur'ān, but revealed books nevertheless, as all references to *zubur* must elicit approval if not veneration; in any case, it is unlikely the Qur'ān would make repeated references to doubtful and false scriptures. It thus becomes obvious upon scrutiny that *Ahl al-Kitāb* in the Qur'ān are not confined to only the Jews and Christians.

On the other hand, those who restrict the category of *Ahl al-Kitāb* to the Jews and Christians quote in authority the Qur'ān (6:156), which declares that Books were revealed *to two groups before*, but the context where this phrase occurs actually questions rather than endorses the spirit of such a limitation. Let us briefly examine the context: The verse (6:156) immediately follows two other verses, one of which affirms the veracity of the Torah that contained guidance and light. The succeeding verse refers to the Qur'ān itself as a *blessed Book* (*kitābun mubārakun*) and an authoritative source. And then comes the verse (6:156): *Lest you should say (think) that Books were sent down to two [groups] of people [only] before us, and for our part, we remained unacquainted (with a revealed Book).* The tone of the discourse here is expressive of the favour bestowed by God upon the Muslims through the revelation of the Qur'ān to them, so that they do not say that God's favour was confined to only two groups of people. Therefore, to give this verse as evidence in support of confining the *Ahl al-Kitāb* to Jews and Christians is unwarranted and leads to an indefensible conclusion. Yet the restrictive interpretation may have been the result, not only of how the scriptural evidence was understood, but also of historical factors, differential practices that Islamic history records on the levying of the poll-tax (*jizya*) on non-Muslims, and its impact on the binary division of the world into Dār al-Islam and Dār al-Harb.

Without wishing to enter into details, it may be said in conclusion that the Qur'ān clearly contains supportive evidence for the more inclusive understanding of *Ahl al-Kitāb*, and the present effort to extend its application to the followers of Buddhism is in line with the tenor of that evidence. The book at hand also reviews a number of other supportive verses in the Qur'ān, side by side with passages from Buddhist scriptures, in an effort to provide theological justification for acceptability and recognition. This effort is to be commended also on grounds of rationality and the spirit of civilizational renewal (*tajdīd*) that may enhance the prospects of cordial relations between the two faith communities. The common ground that is found to exist between Islam and Buddhism elicits recognition and respect of one another on both sides, something so acutely needed at a time when the talk of 'clash of civilizations' has become an unwelcome distraction from the Qur'ānic vision of recognition and friendship (*ta'āruf* – Q.49:13) between the Muslims and other world communities and nations.

Mohammad Hashim Kamali
Chairman and Senior Fellow
International Institute of Advanced Islamic Studies (IAIS)
Malaysia
March 2010

Acknowledgements

I would like to express deep gratitude to the two moving spirits behind this historic initiative to bring Muslims and Buddhists closer together in respect, compassion and mutual understanding: His Holiness the Dalai Lama, and His Royal Highness Prince Ghazi bin Muhammad. May the grace of the All-Compassionate bless their lofty vision and noble intentions with rich fruit in the barely cultivated but immensely fertile common ground upon which these two great traditions stand.

I must also humbly and thankfully acknowledge the inestimable help given to me by Richard Weingarten in regard to the Buddhist side of this book. After having read my first draft, he not only made several important comments and corrections, but also directed me to a whole range of key Buddhist texts which were most pertinent to the central arguments being advanced here. I would also like to thank Paul Towsey for reading through the initial draft of the text and for making some very helpful comments.

Special heartfelt thanks go to the superb editorial team at Fons Vitae: Gray Henry, Neville Blakemore, Eli Brown, Anne Ogden, Valerie Turner and Uzma Husaini, all of whom worked on this text with both meticulous care and palpable concern. It has been a delight working with such a dedicated group of people.

Reza Shah-Kazemi
Westerham
April 2010

Common Ground
Between
Islam and Buddhism

Part One
Setting the Scene

This monograph explores the common ground shared by Islam and Buddhism in the domains of spirituality and morality. What is put forward here is a series of reflections in which we have attempted to interpret some central principles of Buddhism in the light of Islamic spirituality, doing so in a manner which we hope will nourish a spirit of mutual understanding and enriching dialogue between the adherents of the two faiths. Through this dialogue some of the affinities between the two traditions might be brought to the fore, and used as the basis for enhancing mutual respect between Muslims and Buddhists. However great—and indeed irreducible—be the differences between the two traditions on the level of formal doctrine, ritual practice and spiritual 'style', there does appear to be much in the way of spiritual and ethical affinity between the two traditions. These affinities, we argue, reveal a common ground which would remain hidden if we were to restrict ourselves to a comparative analysis of dogma and ritual; such an analysis would highlight instead the vast differences between the two traditions. The affinities to which we draw attention here are not, however, intended to obscure the differences; on the contrary, we start from the premise that these differences should be unabashedly asserted as expressions of the uniqueness of each religion, and not tacitly denied in the quest for spiritual commonalities. Difference and distinctiveness of religious forms are thus to be respected, possibly even celebrated, rather than wished away out of ecumenical politesse. However, in this essay we are concerned not so much with the differences between the two traditions, which are self-evident, but with spiritual affinities, conceptual resonances and common aspirations, which are not.

Beyond the Letter to the Spirit

Our aim in this dialogue is to be as inclusive as possible, both as regards 'the other' and as regards our own tradition. This means that we are not just reaching out to Buddhists, inviting them to consider the Islamic tradition from the perspectives offered here; it also means that we wish to explain some central concepts of Buddhism to Muslims who may not be familiar with this tradition, and are interested in increasing their knowledge of it. Given our intention to be inclusive, we

1

will aim to base discussion as much as possible on the verses of the Holy Qur'ān and the authenticated sayings of the Prophet (peace and blessings be upon him and his family)—even while plumbing some of the deeper, unarticulated implications of commonly held ideas and practices, for it is in this process of exploring the spiritual dynamics underlying fundamental tenets of belief that some of the most striking analogies and affinities between the two faiths are revealed. We are aiming here at commonalities on the level of the spirit of the two traditions, rather than pretending that any unity on the level of the 'letter' of the formal dogmas can be achieved. It would be a mistake to compare Buddhist doctrine to the Islamic creed as if the two were situated on the same plane of thought. They are not. The dogmas in Islam play a very different role within the configuration of Islamic thought and praxis from that played by the doctrines of Buddhism within the Buddhist traditions Indeed, doctrines play different roles even within the diverse Buddhist traditions themselves: what 'doctrine' means for a Zen Buddhist is very different from what it means for a Theravadin Buddhist.

However, if we start by making a distinction between the doctrinal creed (*'aqīda*) of Islam and the spiritual wisdom (*ma'rifa*) nourished within its framework, we may come closer to appreciating the ways in which the two traditions might be compared. *Ma'rifa* pertains to the subtleties of the heart, to inward contemplative states, to mystical experience; *'aqīda* pertains to the beliefs which form the bases of salvation in the Hereafter, and at the same time, serve as the foundation and framework for those spiritual experiences in this world. Most, if not all, of the Buddha's teachings should in fact be situated on the level of what is called *ma'rifa* in Islam, and not on that of *'aqīda*; if we focus on this dimension of spiritual wisdom, then the correspondences between his teachings and the spirit of the Islamic tradition will come into view. Since the doctrines expounding the dimension of *ma'rifa* in Islam are in complete harmony with the essential sources of the Islamic revelation—the Qur'ān and the Prophetic Sunna, upon which they are but commentaries and elaborations—it follows that making an effort to understand Buddhist doctrine in the light of Islamic spirituality helps us to see the underlying common ground between Buddhism and the Islamic tradition per se, and not just between Buddhism and Islamic spirituality. Thus, the affinities revealed on the level of the Spirit will inevitably have some impact on our perception of the gap separating the two faiths on the level of formal dogma. The gap will remain, but will render the two traditions less incommensurable, given the correspondences and resonances glimpsed or intuited on the level of the Spirit.

In strictly theological terms, then, it is clear that the two traditions diverge radically, and any attempt to force some convergence on this plane is bound to fail. To begin with, it is arguable whether one can even speak about a formal discipline of 'theology'—'knowledge of God'—within Buddhism, whereas in Islam, however great be the diversity of different schools of theology, there is an identifiable core of beliefs about God with which all of these schools can easily identify. However, it is possible to speak about the ultimate Reality without doing so from a theological perspective; 'theology' in the strict sense of 'knowledge of God', will be unavoidable, but it will be not scholastic but mystical theology with which we shall engage. If one's focus is on the spiritual domain, a common ground may well be discovered, even on the highest planes, dealing with 'God', the Absolute, or ultimate Reality. Such spiritual affinity, indeed, will be all the more striking against the backdrop of theological incompatibility.

It might be asked from an Islamic point of view whether we are justified in attempting to go beyond, or to bracket out, formal theology in the name of spirituality, metaphysics or mysticism. We would respond with the words of one of the greatest spiritual authorities of Islam, whom we shall cite extensively in this essay, the great 'renewer' (*mujaddid*) of his age, Abū Hāmid al-Ghazālī (d.1111): the science of theology (*kalām*), he says, is restricted in its scope to the outward aspects of the formal creed (*al-'aqīda*); it cannot attain 'spiritual knowledge (*ma'rifa*) of God, His qualities and His acts'. Theology, he argues, is in fact more like 'a veil' obscuring this knowledge. 'The only way to attain this spiritual knowledge is through inner effort (*mujāhada*), which God has established as the prelude to integral guidance'.[1]

In his famous autobiographical work, *al-Munqidh min al-dalāl*

---

1. *Ihyā' 'ulūm al-dīn* (Beirut: Dār al-Jīl, 1992), p. 34; see the English translation of Nabih Amin Faris, *The Book of Knowledge* (Lahore: Sh. Muhammad Ashraf, 1970), (rpr), p. 55, which we have not followed. It is true that al-Ghazālī himself wrote theological treatises, and in his last major work, *al-Mustasfā min 'ilm al-'usūl*, he refers to theology as the 'most exalted science'. But this, it seems, is so in relation to the science of jurisprudence and its various branches, since *al-Mustasfā* addresses the principles of jurisprudence. Eric Ormsby sums up well al-Ghazālī's fundamental attitude to theology: 'it was a weapon, essential for defending the truths of the faith, but not an instrument by which truth itself could be found ...

3

('The Deliverer From Error'), he is even more explicit about the fact that the surest path to the Truth is the mystical one:

> I learnt with certainty that it is above all the mystics who walk on the road of God; their life is the best life, their method, the soundest method, their character the purest character; indeed, were the intellect of the intellectuals and the learning of the learned and the scholarship of the scholars, who are versed in the profundities of revealed truth, brought together in the attempt to improve the life and character of the mystics, they would find no way of doing so; for to the mystics, all movement and rest, whether external and internal, brings illumination derived from the light of the lamp of prophetic revelation.[2]

The mystical or spiritual discipline of *ma'rifa*, pertains to the domain of ultimate principles, a domain which goes beyond the level of dogmatic theology. It does not contradict the formal dogmas of Islam, but rather constitutes their dimension of inner mystical depth and transformative spiritual power, bringing 'illumination from the light of prophetic revelation'. As was stated above, Islamic spirituality does nothing but bring to light the essential nature and deepest meaning of the Islamic revelation. It does so not by contradicting formal theological dogmas, and the faculty of reason proportioned to them, but by plumbing the hidden depths of those dogmas, by means of the spiritual faculty of the heart. As such, *ma'rifa* calls out for spiritual intuition and not simply rational cognition, whence the stress by al-Ghazālī on 'inner effort'. Such effort implies a range of spiritual disciplines, centering on prayer, fasting and purification of the heart and soul from all vices. From the perspectives opened up by these disciplines, the crucial relationship between metaphysics and ethics will be observed; and a perception of this inner nexus between spirituality and morality in Islam can help us to perceive commonalities and affinities with the Buddhist spiritual and ethical tradition.

The aim here, then, is to engage in a dialogue which is focused on spiritual affinities, while remaining keenly aware of fundamental

---

it demolishes but it does not build.' Eric Ormsby, *Ghazali—The Revival of Islam* (Oxford: Oneworld, 2008), p. 64.

2. Translated by W. Montgomery Watt, *The Faith and Practice of Al-Ghazali* (London: George Allen & Unwin, 1953), p. 60. Translation modified.

differences of accentuation, as well as the unbridgeable gap which separates the two traditions in their fundamental creedal structures. This kind of dialogue can yield not just philosophical but also spiritual fruit: for it can allow us to understand dimensions of our own intellectual and spiritual traditions more fully, those dimensions which remain either implicit or less stressed in our tradition, and which can be seen more clearly in the light shed by principles which are accentuated in the religion of the other. Without fundamental *differences* between the two faiths, as regards spiritual economy and dialectical style, this function of reciprocal illumination through dialogue is scarcely conceivable; however, without some notion of the common ground shared by the two religions at the transcendent level, it is unlikely that dialogue can go beyond the simple affirmation of shared ethical and social values. For such an affirmation can so easily go hand in hand with distrust, suspicion and condescension vis-à-vis the religion of the other. The religion of the other might be seen as generating positive ethical values despite the religion's falsity, rather than because of the religion's truth.

The question of ultimate truth and reality cannot therefore be left out of any dialogue that wishes to go beyond scratching the surface of ethical agreement. It is for this reason that in what follows we have devoted considerable attention to the question of the supposed 'atheism'—or, more accurately, 'non-theism'—of Buddhism, for it is this apparent denial of God that constitutes one of the greatest obstacles to effective dialogue between the adherents of Buddhism and other religious traditions. We propose that the ultimate Reality affirmed by Buddhism is nothing other than what monotheists refer to as God; or more precisely, in Islamic terms, to the Essence (*al-Dhāt*) of God. In Muslim theology, *Allāh* comprises diverse qualities/attributes; many of these 'Names', will evidently be quite alien and indeed incomprehensible to the Buddhist intellectual tradition. But when attention is directed to the Essence of *Allāh*, and some of the essential attributes of *Allāh*, such as *al-Haqq* ('the Real' or 'the True') then it becomes possible to discern some common ground between the two faiths on the transcendent plane. The Name *al-Haqq*, as we shall argue below, might be translated into Buddhist terms as *Dharma*. In Arabic, the word *haqq* comprises not only the ideas of truth and reality, but also, that of 'right', that which is 'due'. Therefore the notions of duty, law and propriety are also implied in this polyvalent concept, such notions going to the heart of the meaning of *dharma*. However, at the highest level, the *Dharma* is also identified with absolute Truth, absolute Reality. Recognition of this kind of conceptual affinity at the metaphysical level can help bring the two traditions into harmony, however much the orthodox or conventional frameworks of the two traditions contradict each other.

To speak of orthodoxy calls for the following remark. The definition of 'orthodoxy' in Islam derives not from some official magisterium but from the Qur'ān and the Prophetic Sunna; the question of who is and who is not 'orthodox' in terms of these two sources is resolved by the consensus of the learned (*al-'ulamā'*) in any given period. In our times, Muslim orthodoxy has received its broadest ever definition, thanks to the collective *fatwā* of the leading scholars of Islam issued in Amman in July 2005.[3] This fatwā recognized eight schools of law as being orthodox: the four Sunni schools (Hanafi, Shafi'i, Maliki, Hanbali), the two principal Shi'i schools (Ja'fari and Zaydi), and the Ibadi and Zahiri schools.

When we address Buddhism, however, we are compelled to acknowledge that there is no analogous, clearly definable normative tradition of dogmatically defined orthodoxy. Even referring to Buddhism as a 'religion' comparable to monotheistic religions is problematic. Buddhism is more a network of spiritual schools of thought and praxis than a unified religion, the numerous branches not only differing widely on the level of doctrine and rituals, but also occasionally engaging in considerable mutual ostracism. All Buddhist schools are however united on the fundamental teachings of the Buddha, as expressed in the Pali canon; for this reason we have tried to engage with this body of teachings as much as possible, in addition to addressing some perspectives expressed in later schools, which more clearly manifest similarities with Islamic doctrines.

Even though we have restricted our reflections to a few principles within a few of the Buddhist traditions—given our own scholarly limitations—we are nonetheless addressing the main schools of thought within Buddhism, and invite all of them to engage in this dialogue: the two principal branches of this tradition: the Theravada ('Way of the Elders'), and the Mahayana ('Greater Vehicle'), this latter comprising such schools as the Madhyamaka ('Middle Path' founded by Nāgārjūna, ca. 2nd century CE)[4], Yogacara (founded by

---

3. See http://www.ammanmessage.com.
4. Scholars are divided over the question of the dates of the birth and death of this immensely influential figure in Buddhism, considered by many within the tradition

the brothers Asanga and Vasubandhu, ca. 4/5th century CE); the Chinese Chan school (founded by Bodhidharma, migrating from India to China in the late 5th century CE; this is the basis of the Zen school in Japan[5]); the Pure Land school, again rooted in Indian Mahayana texts but articulated in China (as the Ching-t'u tsung school), and in Japan (as Jodo Shin); and finally the traditions of the Vajrayāna ('Adamantine Way' also known as Tantric Buddhism, which found its principal flowering in Tibet; known also in Japan as 'Shingon'). This list is not intended to be exhaustive; it merely highlights some of the main schools within Buddhism to which reference will be made here.

It is our hope that in the light of these affinities the adherents of each religion might come to appreciate more deeply the value of the religion of the other, and to place the profound differences between their traditions within a context defined by mutual respect: it might help Muslims to see Buddhism as a true religion or *dīn*, and Buddhists to see Islam as an authentic *dharma*. This mutual recognition, alone, is of immense benefit, and can only reinforce the kind of harmony which is so much more easily attained on the level of ethics and morality.

A Glance at History

Throughout Islamic history, Buddhists—together with Hindus and Zoroastrians, not to mention other religious groups—were regarded by Muslims not as pagans, polytheists, or atheists, but as followers of an authentic religion, and thus to be granted official *dhimmī* status, that is, they were to be granted official protection by the state

---

as 'the second Buddha' (see David J. Kalupahana, *Nāgārjuna—The Philosophy of the Middle Way* (State University of New York Press, 1986), p. 2). The most that one can say, according to Joseph Walser, is that 'there is no real evidence that Nāgārjuna lived before 100 B.C.E. or after 265 C.E.'. *Nāgārjuna in Context* (New York: Columbia University Press, 2005), p. 63.

5. Zen is an abbreviated form of *Zenna*, as Ch'an is of *Ch'anna*, both being derived from the Sanskrit *Dhyāna*, meaning meditation. According to Daihetz Suzuki, Zen is 'no doubt the native product of the Chinese mind'; it is 'the Chinese way of applying the doctrine of enlightenment in our practical life'. D.T. Suzuki, *Essays in Zen Buddhism* (London: Rider & Company, 1970), vol. 1, pp. 36, 39. The origin of Zen is regarded as the Buddha's famous, wordless, 'flower sermon', in which the Buddha said nothing, and only held up a flower. One disciple understood: Mahākasyapa; and he is regarded as the first master of 'Zen', though the school was to flourish only several hundred years later. The Buddha is reported to have said: 'I have the most precious treasure, spiritual and transcendental, which this moment I hand over to you, O venerable Mahākasyapa.' See ibid., vol. 1, pp. 60, 167.

authorities: any violation of their religious, social or legal rights was subject to the 'censure' (*dhimma*) of the Muslim authorities, who were charged with the protection of these rights.

It is instructive to glance at the roots of this Muslim appraisal of the religio-juridical status of Buddhism. One of the earliest and most decisive encounters between Islam and Buddhism on the soil of India took place during the short but successful campaign of the young Umayyad general, Muhammad b. Qāsim in Sind, launched in 711. During the conquest of this predominantly Buddhist province, he received petitions from the indigenous Buddhists and Hindus in the important city of Brahmanabad regarding the restoration of their temples and the upholding of their religious rights generally. He consulted his superior, the governor of Kufa, Hajjāj b. Yūsuf, who in turn consulted his religious scholars. The result of these deliberations was the formulation of an official position which was to set a decisive precedent of religious tolerance for the ensuing centuries of Muslim rule in India. Hajjāj wrote to Muhammad b. Qāsim a letter which was translated into what became known as the 'Brahmanabad settlement':

'The request of the chiefs of Brahmanabad about the building of Budh and other temples, and toleration in religious matters, is just and reasonable. I do not see what further rights we can have over them beyond the usual tax. They have paid homage to us and have undertaken to pay the fixed tribute [*jizya*] to the Caliph. Because they have become *dhimmī*s we have no right whatsoever to interfere in their lives and property. Do permit them to follow their own religion. No one should prevent them.'[6]

The Arab historian, al-Balādhurī, quotes Muhammad b. Qāsim's famous statement made at Alor (Arabised as 'al-Rūr'), a city besieged for a week, and then taken without force, according to strict terms: there was to be no bloodshed, and the Buddhist faith would not be opposed. Muhammad b. Qāsim was reported to have said:

The temples [lit. al-Budd, but referring to the temples of the Buddhists and the Hindus, as well as the Jains] shall be treated by us as if they were the churches of the Christians, the synagogues of the Jews, and the fire temples of the Magians.[7]

---

6. *Chachnamah Retold—An Account of the Arab Conquest of Sindh*, Gobind Khushalani (New Delhi: Promilla, 2006), p. 156

7. Abū al-Hasan al-Balādhurī, *Futūḥ al-buldān* (Beirut: Maktaba al-Hilāl, 1988), pp. 422–423.

It is thus not surprising to read, in the same historian's work, that when Muhammad b. Qāsim died, 'The people of India wept at the death of Muhammad, and made an image of him at Kīraj'.[8]

Although subsequent Muslim rulers varied in their degree of fidelity to this precedent establishing the principle of religious tolerance in India,[9] the point being made here is more theological than political. What is to be stressed is that Buddhists were, in principle, to be granted the same religious and legal recognition as fellow monotheists, the Jews and the Christians, or the 'People of the Book' (*Ahl al-Kitāb*). The implication of this act of recognition is clear: the religion these Buddhists followed was not analogous to the pagan polytheistic religions, whose adherents were not granted such privileges. Rather, as a community akin to the 'People of the Book', they were regarded, implicitly if not explicitly, as recipients of an authentic divine revelation.

It may be argued, however, that granting Buddhists legal recognition was in fact more political than theological; that the instinctive response of Hajjāj and his general stemmed more from hard-headed pragmatism than subtle theological reflection. While such pragmatism no doubt played a role in this historic decision, the point to be made is this: that the scholars of Islam did not (and still do not) regard this 'pragmatic' policy as violating or compromising any fundamental theological principle of Islam. Pragmatism and principle

---

8. Ibid., p. 424. See for further discussion, S.M. Ikram, *History of Muslim Civilization in India and Pakistan* (Lahore: Institute of Islamic Culture, 1989).

9. One cannot overlook such acts as the destruction of the monastery at Valabhi by the Abbsasid army in 782. But, to quote the Buddhist scholar, Dr Alexander Berzin, 'The destruction at Valabhi ... was an exception to the general religious trends and official policies of the early Abbasid period. There are two plausible explanations for it. It was either the work of a militant fanatic general acting on his own, or a mistaken operation ordered because of the Arabs' confusing the local "white-clad" Jains with supporters of Abu Muslim and then not differentiating the Buddhists from the Jains. It was not part of a *jihad* specifically against Buddhism.' See his 'The Historical Interaction between the Buddhist and Islamic Cultures before the Mongol Empire' in his 'The Berzin Archives—the Buddhist Archives of Dr Alexander Berzin' (http://www.berzinarchives.com/web/en/archives/e-books/unpublished_manuscripts/historical_interaction/pt2/history_cultures_10.html). Any other acts of unprincipled violence by rogue Muslim generals, should likewise be seen as contrary to 'the general religious trends and official policies' of Muslim states acting in accordance with Islamic precepts. These acts are political exceptions which prove the religious rule: the rights of Hindus and Buddhists, as *dhimmī*s, were sacrosanct.

went hand in hand. The implication of granting Buddhists legal recognition, political protection and religious tolerance is that the spiritual path and moral code of the Buddhist faith derive from an authentic revelation of God. If this be disputed by Muslims, then the historical practice of granting Buddhists *dhimmī* status will be seen to be nothing more than 'Realpolitik', at best, or a betrayal of certain theological principles, at worst: one would be guilty of according religious legitimacy to a false religion. We would argue, on the contrary, that the Buddhists were recognized—in an as it were existential, intuitive, largely unarticulated manner—by Muslims as followers of an authentic faith, even if this faith appeared to contradict Islam in certain major respects; that the early Muslims in their encounters with Buddhism observed sufficient 'family resemblances' between Buddhism and the 'People of the Book' for them to feel justified in extending to Buddhists the same legal and religious rights granted to the 'People of the Book'; that the 'pragmatic' decision of the politicians and generals was actually in harmony with the Islamic revelation, despite the reservations, refutations or denunciations stemming from popular Muslim prejudice, and despite the paucity of scholarly works by Muslims making doctrinally explicit what was implied in the granting of *dhimmī* status to Buddhists.

It would be useful to explore further the implications of this early Muslim response to Buddhism, and to provide a more explicit theological—or spiritual—justification for this response, which formed the basis of the official policy of tolerance of Buddhism by Muslims world-wide. The consequences for dialogue will be self-evident. If Buddhists are recognized as akin to the 'People of the Book', then they are implicitly to be included in the spectrum of 'saved' communities, as expressed in the following verse, one of the most universal verses of the Qur'ān: *Truly those who believe and those who are Jews, and the Christians and the Sabeans—whoever believes in God and the Last Day and performs virtuous acts—for such, their reward is with their Lord, no fear or grief will befall them* (2:62; repeated almost verbatim at 5:69).

One of our aims in this essay is to make explicit that which in large part has hitherto remained implicit: if Buddhists, like Jews, Christians and Sabeans, are to be treated as 'People of the Book', and thus placed within the sphere of those believers mentioned in this verse, it should be possible for Muslims to recognize Buddhist doctrines as expressing 'belief in God and the Last Day', and to recognize the acts prescribed by Buddhism as 'virtuous acts'. Indeed, in light of the verses cited above, it should be possible to demonstrate that the essence of the Buddhist message is at one with the immutable and unique message of all the Messengers: *And We sent no Messenger before you but We inspired him* [saying]*: There is no God save Me, so worship Me* (21:25); this verse confirms the uniqueness of the message: *Nothing is said unto you* [Muhammad] *but what was said unto the Messengers before you* (41:43).

If it cannot be shown that the essence of the Buddha's message is at one with that of the message of the Qur'ān, it might be possible at least to demonstrate that it is 'like' it: *And if they believe in the like of that which ye believe, then are they rightly guided ...* (2:137). If even this cannot be done, then one is deprived of much of the religio-legal ground, or the spiritual logic, of the conventional Muslim practice of granting *dhimmī* status to Buddhists. For this status must imply that, unlike man-made paganism, the religion practised by them is—or at least was[10]—an authentic one, revealed by God.

Let us also note that there is in the juristic tradition a lively debate about whether those communities to whom the *dhimmī* status was granted should also be regarded as *Ahl al-Kitāb* in the full sense. The great jurist, al-Shafi'i, founder of one of the four schools of law in Sunni Islam, asserted that the Qur'ānic references to the scriptures of Abraham and Moses (*suhufi Ibrāhīm wa Mūsā*; 87:19), and the scriptures of the ancients (*zubur al-awwalīn*; 26:196) can be used as the basis for arguing that God revealed scriptures other than those specifically mentioned in the Qur'ān. He concludes that Zoroastrians, for example, can also be included in the category of

---

10. This reservation is important, for the overwhelming majority of Muslim scholars accept that the 'People of the Book' are undoubtedly recipients of an authentic revelation which inaugurates their respective traditions; but that they have not been faithful to that revelation, whether through deliberate distortion of their scriptures (*tahrīf*) or through a degeneration which is the ransom of the passage of time. The Buddha himself referred to the inevitability of such a degeneration in numerous prophecies, which gave rise to further prophecies five centuries after his passing away. According to Edward Conze, 'Prophecies dating from the beginning of the Christian era have given 2,500 years as the duration of the teaching of the Buddha Śākyamuni.' E. Conze, *Buddhism—A Short History* (Oxford: Oneworld, 2000), p. 141. What matters in an exploration of common ground is the concordance on the level of principles, the extent to which these principles are practised is a different question altogether.

Ahl al-Kitāb, and not treated only as a 'protected community', *Ahl al-dhimma*.[11]

Qur'ānic Premises of Dialogue

Our approach to interfaith dialogue is based explicitly on the following key Qur'ānic verses regarding dialogue:[12]

> *O mankind, truly We have created you male and female, and have made you nations and tribes that you may know one another...* (49:13)

> *And of His signs is the creation of the heavens and the earth, and the differences of your languages and colours. Indeed, herein are signs for those who know.* (30:22)

> *Call unto the way of thy Lord with wisdom and fair exhortation, and hold discourse with them in the finest manner.* (16:125)

The kaleidoscope of human variety and difference is a stimulus to knowledge—knowledge of the other and knowledge of oneself. This seeking of knowledge will be successful if dialogue be based on what is 'finest' in one's own faith, and in the faith of those with whom one is in dialogue:

> *And do not hold discourse with the People of the Book except in that which is finest, save with those who do wrong. And say: We believe in that which has been revealed to us and revealed to you. Our God and your God is one, and unto Him we surrender.* (29:46)

Here, mention is made explicitly of the 'People of the Book'—the Jews and Christians, but, as we shall see, the boundaries defining this category are flexible and not fixed. All revealed religions can be placed within this category, which thereby comes to embrace the whole of humanity, given that no human community has been deprived of revelation. The following verses uphold this key premise of dialogue, stressing the inner unity of the message of religion *per*

---

11. Yohanan Friedmann, *Tolerance and Coercion in Islam—Interfaith Relations in the Muslim Tradition* (Cambridge: Cambridge University Press, 2003), p. 81, citing al-Shafi'i's *Kitab al-umm*, 4/245 et passim.

12. All translations from the Qur'ān are based on M.M. Pickthall's translation, with minor modifications.

se, on the one hand, and the outer diversity of the forms clothing this unique message, on the other:[13]

> • *For every community there is a Messenger.* (10:47)

> • *For each of you* [communities] *We have established a Law and a Way. And had God willed, He could have made you one community. But in order that He might try you by that which He has given you* [He has made you as you are]. *So vie with one another in good works. Unto God you will all return, and He will inform you of that about which you differed.* (5:48)

> • *And We never sent a messenger save with the language of his people, so that he might make* [Our message] *clear to them.* (14:4)

> • *Truly We inspire you, as We inspired Noah, and the prophets after him, as We inspired Abraham and Ishmael and Isaac and Jacob and the tribes, and Jesus and Job and Jonah and Aaron and Solomon, and as We bestowed unto David the Psalms; and Messengers We have mentioned to you before, and Messengers We have not mentioned to you.* (4:163–164)

> • *And We sent no Messenger before you but We inspired him* [saying]: *There is no God save Me, so worship Me.* (21:25)

> • *Naught is said unto you* [Muhammad] *but what was said unto the Messengers before you.* (41:43)

On the basis of these premises, it should be possible to mount a serious argument in favour of the proposition that the Buddha was a Messenger, inspired by God with a message which was destined to become the basis of a global religious community. He is not mentioned by name in the Qur'ān, but in light of what is said in 4:164, one can argue that the Buddha could well be one of the Messengers not explicitly mentioned in the Islamic revelation. This argument is strengthened when one considers that over ten percent of the inhabitants of the globe belong to the community inaugurated by the

---

13. See our *The Other in the Light of the One—The Holy Qur'ān and Interfaith Dialogue* (Cambridge: Islamic Texts Society, 2006), for elaboration of this perspective.

Buddha; if 'for every community there is a Messenger', it would appear logical to conclude that the Buddha is the Messenger for this vast community of believers.

The Buddha as Messenger

One of the epithets by which the Buddha described himself is *Tathāgatā*, which means the one who has 'thus come' and also 'thus gone'. In their authoritative translation of one of the major scriptural compilations of the Pali canon, the *Majjhima Nikāya* ('Middle Length Discourses'), Bhikku Nanamoli and Bikkhu Bodhi explain the dual meaning as follows: 'The Pali commentators explain the word as meaning "thus come" (*tathā āgata*) and "thus gone" (*tathā gata*), that is, the one who *comes* into our midst bearing the message of deathlessness to which he has *gone* by his own practice of the path.'[14] It is worth quoting further from this description of the Buddha's function, as it reinforces the argument made above, that the Buddha is indeed one of the Messengers sent by God to humanity: 'He is not merely a wise sage or a benevolent moralist but the latest in the line of Fully Enlightened Ones, each of whom arises singly in an age of spiritual darkness, discovers the deepest truths about the nature of existence, and establishes a Dispensation (*sāsana*) through which the path to deliverance again becomes accessible to the world.'

The essence of this dispensation is derived from the Buddha's enlightenment, referred to as Nibbāna (Sanskrit: Nirvāna), and also as Dhamma (Sanskrit: *Dharma*). This Nibbāna is described in the following terms, all of which are juxtaposed with their opposites, so many forms of bondage, from which the Buddha said he sought—and found—deliverance:

- unborn supreme security from bondage
- unageing supreme security from bondage
- unailing supreme security from bondage
- deathless supreme security from bondage
- sorrowless supreme security from bondage
- undefiled supreme security from bondage[15]

---

14. *The Middle Length Discourses of the Buddha—A Translation of the Majjhima Nikāya* (trs. Bhikku Nanamoli & Bhikku Bodhi) (Oxford: The Pali Texts Society, 1995), p. 24.

15. Ibid., 26:18, pp. 259–260.

The Buddha continues to describe this enlightenment in terms of the 'Dhamma'—as we shall see below, this term can be translated by such terms as 'law', 'way' and 'norm' on the one hand; and as ultimate truth and reality, on the other. So the enlightenment and the way to enlightenment are virtually synonymous. The Dhamma, then, is described by the Buddha as 'profound, hard to see and hard to understand, peaceful and sublime, unattainable by mere reasoning, subtle, to be experienced by the wise'. The essence of the enlightenment thus remains incommunicable, it can only be 'experienced' by the wise, and is 'unattainable by mere reasoning'. According to the Diamond Sūtra: 'truth is uncontainable and inexpressible'.[16] So only the means by which enlightenment can be attained are communicable. This communicable content of the enlightenment experience is summed up in the 'Four Noble Truths'. It is the declaration of these truths that sets the 'wheel of the *Dharma*' turning at the first sermon delivered by the Budhha, to five monks in the Deer Park at Isipatana, Benares. These truths are: the fact of suffering; the origin of suffering; the cessation of suffering; the way leading to the cessation of suffering. They are explained in various places in different ways, one succinct presentation of them is given in the following passage. The Buddha asks: 'What is suffering?':

> Birth is suffering; ageing is suffering; sickness is suffering; death is suffering; sorrow, lamentation, pain, grief, and despair are suffering; not to obtain what one wants is suffering; in short, the five aggregates[17] affected by clinging are suffering. This is called suffering.
>
> And what is the origin of suffering? It is craving, which brings renewal of being, is accompanied by delight and lust, and delights in this and that; that is, craving for sensual pleasures, craving for being, and craving for non-being. This is called the origin of suffering.
>
> And what is the cessation of suffering? It is the remainderless fading away and ceasing, the giving up, relinquish-

---

16. *The Diamond Sutra and The Sutra of Hui-Neng*, tr. A.F. Price & Wong Moulam (Boston: Shambhala, 1990), p. 24.

17. These aggregates (*skandha*s) are: material form, feeling, perception, mental formations, consciousness. See *The Middle Length Discourses*, op. cit., pp. 26–27 for an explanation of these aggregates by Bhikku Nanamoli and Bhikku Bodhi. See also Thich Nhat Hanh, *The Heart of the Buddha's Teaching* (Berkeley: Parallax Press, 1988), ch. 23, 'The Five Aggregates', pp. 164–171.

ing, letting go, and rejecting of that same craving. This is called the cessation of suffering.

And what is the way leading to the cessation of suffering? It is just this Noble Eightfold Path; that is, right view, right intention, right speech, right action, right livelihood, right effort, right mindfulness, right concentration. This is called the way leading to the cessation of suffering.[18]

It is to be noted that the Qur'ānic definition of salvation in Islam is directly connected with the cessation of suffering; it is from the suffering of hell, precisely, that one is in fact 'saved': *Truly those who believe and those who are Jews, and the Christians and the Sabeans—whoever believes in God and the Last Day and performs virtuous acts—for such, their reward is with their Lord, no fear or grief will befall them* (2:62; repeated almost verbatim at 5:69). One might ask whether the two types of suffering are situated on the same plane: whereas the Muslim idea of avoiding suffering is connected to the avoidance of perpetual torment in hell, the Buddha's message appears to pertain only to the cessation of suffering in this world. However, there is certainly an 'eschatological' aspect to the Buddha's message (just as inversely, there is a terrestrial aspect to the cessation of suffering in Islam), and this is made clear in many sermons where posthumous existences are referred to in terms identifiable as 'heavenly' and 'hellish', depending on the nature of the deeds performed here on earth. Indeed, the principle of accountability, and of tasting the fruits hereafter only of one's actions herebelow, was central to the Buddha's own enlightenment. Describing the various phases of his enlightenment, he speaks as follows:

When my concentrated mind was thus purified, bright, unblemished, rid of imperfection, malleable, wieldy, steady, and attained to imperturbability, I directed it to knowledge of the passing away and reappearance of beings. With the divine eye, which is purified and surpasses the human, I saw beings passing away and reappearing, inferior and superior, fair and ugly, fortunate and unfortunate. I understood how beings pass on according to their actions thus: 'These unworthy beings who were ill conducted in body, speech and

---

18. Ibid., 9.15–18, pp. 134–135. We have inserted all eight dimensions of the Path, whereas the translators had mentioned only two, separated by an ellipsis, given the fact that the list had appeared several times in this Sutta already.

mind, revilers of noble ones, wrong in their views, giving effect to wrong view in their actions, on the dissolution of the body, after death, have reappeared in a state of deprivation, in a bad destination, in perdition, even in hell; but those worthy being who were well conducted in body, speech and mind, not revilers of noble ones, right in their views, giving effect to their right views in their actions, on the dissolution of the body, after death, have reappeared in a good destination, even in the heavenly world.' Thus with the divine eye, which is purified and surpasses the human, I saw beings passing away and reappearing inferior and superior, fair and ugly, fortunate and unfortunate, and I understood how beings pass on according to their actions.[19]

The concrete reality of the principle of *karma*, of concordant actions and reactions, was thus brought home to the Buddha as part of his original enlightenment, whence the repeated insistence on the necessity of ethical propriety, manifested through an adherence to the Noble Eightfold Path. The ethical content of the Buddha's message is thus strikingly similar to that which one finds in Islam. Not only are there numerous correspondences between Islamic ethics and each of the aspects of the Noble Eightfold Path, but also as regards the fundamental determinant of one's life hereafter, there is an undeniable similarity, centred on the nature of one's actions. 'O My servants', God says in a *hadīth qudsī* (divine utterance), 'it is but your deeds that I reckon up for you and then recompense you for.'[20]

There are no doubt profound differences between the two faiths as regards the way in which this principle of posthumous recompense or ultimate accountability operates: in Islam, there is belief in a Personal Divinity, God as the Judge, who weighs up our deeds, and in Buddhism the principle of *karma* is strictly impersonal. Nonetheless, the incompatibility between the two perspectives pertains to the *operation* of the principle of accountability, and not to the principle itself. In fact, one observes within Islam both modes of operation. The conception of God as 'personal' Judge is obviously predominant in the Qur'ān; but the complementary principle is by no means absent: an intimation of the Bud-

19. Ibid., 4.29, pp. 105–106.

20. Recorded in Muslim, Tirmidhī and Ibn Mājah. See for the English and Arabic text, *Forty Hadith Qudsi*, selected and translated by E. Ibrahim and D. Johnson-Davies (Beirut: Dar al-Koran al-Kareem, 1980), p. 84.

dhist 'impersonal' perspective is given in the following verses of the Qur'ān:

> *And every man's augury have We fastened to his own neck, and We shall bring forth for him on the Day of Resurrection a book which he will find wide open.* [It will be said to him] *'Read your book, your own soul suffices as reckoner against yourself this day'* (17:13–14).

Even if there are dozens of other verses in which God as Judge is deemed to be the determinant of one's fate in the Hereafter, this single verse shows that the essential principle of accountability in the Hereafter can be expressed in different ways. The theistically conceived 'Judge' can be seen, from a Buddhist point of view, as one way of expressing the objectivity of the principle of cosmic recompense; while *karma* can be conceived, from a Muslim point of view, as one way of expressing the principle according to which the Judge evaluates all deeds.[21] Moreover, as will be seen in the section on compassion, in both traditions there is a principle which transcends the cosmic chain of cause and effect, and this is divine mercy.

The affinity remains, therefore, on the level of principle, and this can help reinforce the basic argument sketched out above, and which we hope to flesh out in what follows: that there are enough resemblances between the two faiths to enable Muslims to affirm that Buddhists are guided by a true religion, one which is 'like' Islam in the sense intended by the words of the following verse:

> *And if they believe in the like of that which ye believe, then are they rightly guided ...* (2:137).

It should be noted that this verse comes immediately after one of the most comprehensive descriptions of the scope of the prophetic mission—several prophets being named specifically, and then all prophets being referred to in general:

> *Say: We believe in God and that which is revealed unto us and that which was revealed unto Abraham, and Ishmael, and Isaac, and Jacob, and the tribes, and that which Moses and Jesus received, and that which the prophets received*

---

21. See the interesting comparison made by His Holiness, the Dalai Lama, of the Buddhist view of *karma* as opposed to the Christian view of God as Judge, in his *The Good Heart: A Buddhist Perspective on the Teachings of Jesus* (Somerville: Wisdom Publications, 1996), p. 115ff.

from their Lord. We make no distinction between any of them, and unto Him we have surrendered (2:136).

As noted above, verse 2:62 of the Qur'ān teaches us that salvation is dependent upon the realization of three principles: belief in the Absolute, accountability to that Absolute, and virtuous conduct in consequence of these beliefs. At this point it would appear that the Buddha certainly taught the latter two principles; as regards the first, belief in the Absolute, we shall be addressing this below, in chapter 1. If our argument there is valid, then there would appear to be sufficient grounds for asserting that Buddhist beliefs are certainly close enough to Islamic ones to be regarded as authentic guidance: *if they believe in the like of that which ye believe, then are they rightly guided.*

It would be appropriate at this point to proceed with an evaluation of the nature of the Buddha's enlightenment—bearing in mind that the word 'buddha' means 'awakened one'[22]—in the light of the Islamic concept of divine revelation.

Revelation from on High or Within?

'With the divine eye, which is purified and surpasses the human': this phrase, from *The Middle Length Discourses*, cited above, is one of the keys to understanding the Buddha's message and his dialectic. However much be the emphasis on the human aspect of his enlightenment, it is clear from this citation alone—and many more could be given—that it is only something beyond the human and the relative that can give rise to the transcendent perceptions of spiritual realities which constitute the message of the Buddha. In other words, this phrase gives us a clear intimation of the transcendent source of the vision enjoyed by the Buddha, even if in the Buddhist perspective one refuses to name this transcendent source. This refusal stems from a fear of reifying this transcendent source of enlightenment, that is, turning it into an object. For in reality it is the supreme source of all consciousness, which cannot in any way be given a 'name' and a 'form' (*namarupa*) without diminishing one's receptivity to it as the ultimate reality; being the very *substance* of all thought, it cannot

---

22. In certain Mahayana texts, the word 'refers to reality itself, and to people who are awake to reality', according to Thomas Cleary in the introduction to his translation of the seminal Mahayana text, *The Flower Ornament Scripture—A Translation of the Avatamsaka Sutra*, Translated from the Chinese by Thomas Cleary (Boulder & London: Shambhala, 1984), p. 3.

be the *object* of thought. It is nonetheless 'objective' in relation to human subjectivity, and that is why the Buddha refers to the 'divine eye' which surpasses human modes of cognition. The transcendent objectivity of the source of enlightenment reveals itself through and as the immanent consciousness of the one enlightened, the 'Buddha'.

At first sight it may seem that the Islamic conception of prophecy (*nubuwwa*) contradicts the Buddhist conception of enlightenment (*bodhi*). In Islam, the function of prophecy devolves upon particular individuals, chosen by God, and nobody can aspire to the status of prophecy, or participate in its function. In Buddhism, by contrast, it is stated that enlightenment was not bestowed upon the Buddha by any external, objective 'divinity'; it sprang up from his own innermost substance, and his state of enlightenment is attainable by all, in principle. This point of view is succinctly expressed in the following text from the Pali canon:

> Therefore, O Ananda, be ye lamps unto yourselves. Be ye a refuge unto yourselves. Betake yourselves to no external refuge. Hold fast to the Truth as a lamp. Hold fast as a refuge to the Truth …it is they, Ananda, who shall reach the very topmost Height …[23]

The idea of seeking 'no external refuge', and being a refuge unto oneself appears to fly in the face of the Qur'ānic insistence on total dependence upon God and upon His revelation conveyed by His chosen Prophet. Any attempt to be independent is severely censured:

> *Read, in the name of your Lord who created; created man from a clot. Read, and your Lord is most bounteous, He who taught by the Pen; taught man what he knew not. But nay, verily man is rebellious, in that he deems himself independent. Unto your Lord is indeed the Return* (96:1–8).

However, it can be argued that the Buddha's enlightenment comprises two aspects, one of which was proper to him alone, the other which is universally accessible. The first aspect can indeed be regarded as the source of his 'prophecy', to use Islamic terms, the 'message' or *sāsana* which formed the basis of the Buddhist tradi-

---

23. Ananda K. Coomaraswamy, *Buddha and the Gospel of Buddhism* (New Jersey: Citadel Press, 1988), p. 77.

20

tion; in this respect, no other sage or 'prophet' is conceivable in the Buddhist tradition, and none can attain to his status, as regards what in Islam would be called his *risāla*, his message. In regard to the second, the enlightenment he attained was indeed made accessible in principle to all those who followed his teachings; this corresponds to what in Islam is called *walāya*, sanctified consciousness. The Prophet was both *rasūl* and *walī*, Messenger and saint; in respect of the first, his status is unique, and none can aspire to it; as regards the second, one who does not aspire to sanctification is heedless of the meaning of the prophet as role-model and example: *There is indeed for you in the Messenger of God a beautiful exemplar ...* (33:21).

In other words, while the specific message which defines the Prophetic function is indeed bestowed upon him, alone, his sanctity, by contrast, can be the object of the aspiration for all, in principle, who follow his *Sunna*; indeed, emulating the Prophet culminates for the highest saints in a real participation, to some degree at least, in the Prophet's own sanctity, his *walāya* being the source of the *walāya* of the saints. The 'friends of God' (*awliyā' Allāh*) are saints, then, but not prophets. They are enlightened beings, but not messengers of God.

It may be objected here that this enlightenment constitutes, precisely, the revelation experienced by the Buddha, and that this surging up of enlightenment from within cannot be equated with the descent (*tanzīl*) of revelation from on high. In the first case, it would be argued, the knowledge acquired comes from oneself, at however deep a level of consciousness, and is thus subjective; in the second, the knowledge bestowed comes from without, and is thus objective. Moreover, in the one there is no mention of a divinity, only a deeper dimension of the self, whereas in the other, any hint that the revelation has anything to do with the person of the Prophet is heretical.

One can resolve this dilemma with the help of two fundamental principles: one of which we have mentioned above, pertaining to what the Buddha called the 'divine eye', and the other, the fundamental notion of *anattā*, 'no-self'. To address briefly the latter, this doctrine is known as one of the three 'marks' in Buddhist doctrine, the other two being *dukkha* (suffering) and *anicca* (impermanence). These three 'marks' of existence complement the four noble truths, and in particular, explain the mechanism of suffering: that which suffers is not a permanent self, but the various perishable aggregates of which individual beings are composed; these aggregates at-tach themselves to objects which are likewise perishable: their very impermanence ensures that the aggregates of the being attached to them will experience the phenomenon of suffering.

As regards *anattā*, the Buddha explains to his disciple Ananda the meaning of the statement 'The world is empty' in the following way: '… it is empty, Ananda, of a self, or of anything of the nature of a self. And what is it that is thus empty? The five seats of the five senses, and the mind, and the feeling that is related to the mind: all these are void of a self or of anything that is self-like.'[24]

It should be immediately apparent that, in good Buddhist logic, if there is no permanent, abiding 'self', Gautama the man cannot be accused of having brought to the surface of his specific conscious-ness anything residing in the innermost depths of *his self*. As will be seen shortly, a fundamental tenet of Buddhist belief is that all individual *dharma*s are baseless, empty, illusory. This applies, first and foremost to the individual self. Only *The Dharma*, absolutely transcending the individual is real. We say 'absolutely', for the two domains—such and such a *dharma*, on the one hand, and the *Dharma* as such, on the other—are incommensurable; it is like the differ-ence between light and darkness.

If the Buddha's enlightenment taught him that the empirical self is an illusion, the source of that enlightenment cannot pos-sibly be the empirical self, for this self is rendered illusory in the light of that very enlightenment. The relative self cannot reveal the relativity of the self. The 'revelation' of this relativity must, on the contrary, be derived from something absolute, being that which alone can reveal the self to be illusory, and that 'something' abso-lute can only be the objective principle whence all consciousness, life and being flow.[25] This principle must radically transcend the particular man, Gautama Shakyamuni. In other words, we arrive at the inescapable conclusion that Gautama, as a human being, could only have attained his enlightenment by virtue of an objec-tive principle infinitely transcending his own humanity, and that objective principle is the source of all revelation, that which in Islam is called *Allāh*. One can then distinguish between enlight-

---

24. *Samyutta Nikāya*, 4:54, cited in ibid., p. 98.

25. See Marco Pallis, 'Is There Room for Grace in Buddhism?' in his *A Buddhist Spectrum* (London: George Allen & Unwin, 1980), pp. 52–71, for a compelling ar-gument demonstrating that 'grace' is strongly implicit within Buddhist teachings.

enment as such, and the specific contents or the 'message'—the *risāla*—conveyed through that enlightenment, by means of which others can be helped to achieve enlightenment themselves:

> The Conquerors are masters of various and manifold means whereby the Tathāgata reveals the supreme light to the world of gods and men—means adapted to their temperaments and prejudices.[26]

In the light of the above discussion we can interpret this verse from the *Saddharmapundarīka Sūtra* as follows: the revelation of the Tathāgata is the revelation of the Buddha-nature (*Buddhadhātu*), the principle, and not Shakyamuni the man; it is the revelation of the Absolute, which is bestowed upon human communities in the form of a *sāsana* ('dispensation') communicated by an *upāya* ('skilful means') adapted to their conditions. Thomas Cleary, commenting upon the 'infinity and eternity of Buddha', writes as follows: 'enlightened guides present various teachings to people in accord with their needs, potentials and conditions ... This principle of adaptation and specific prescription is known as "skill in means".' This principle reminds one of the Qur'ānic perspective: *And We never sent a messenger save with the language of his people, so that he might make it clear to them* (14:4).

Given these premises, it should be possible for Muslims to mount a serious argument in favour of the proposition that the Buddha was a 'messenger of God', however much such a designation be resisted by Buddhists themselves. By doing so, they will be reflecting the fact that many Buddhists are able to recognize the Prophet Muhammad as one of the individuals in whose mission the function of the *Dharma-kāya*[27] was manifested—even if many Muslims themselves will resist such a designation. According to Suzuki:

> Perceiving an incarnation of the *Dharmakāya* in every spiritual leader regardless of his nationality and professed creed, Mahayanists recognized a Buddha in Socrates, Mohammad, Jesus, Francis of Assisi, Confucius, Laotze, and many others.[28]

---

26. *Saddharmapundarīka Sūtra* 2:36 and 73; cited in Coomaraswamy, *Buddha and the Gospel of Buddhism*, op. cit., p. 159.

27. Literally: the body of the Dharma. We shall be addressing this important concept below.

28. D.T. Suzuki, *Outlines of Mahayana Buddhism*, p. 63; cited in ibid., p. 159.

The Dalai Lama and the Dynamics of Dialogue

Finally, let us return to the Qur'ānic verse cited above, the importance of which for the principle and the practice of interfaith dialogue cannot be over-estimated:

> For each of you [communities] We have established a Law
> and a Way. And had God willed, He could have made you
> one community. But in order that He might try you by that
> which He has given you [He has made you as you are]. So
> vie with one another in good works. Unto God you will all
> return, and He will inform you of that about which you dif-
> fered. (5:48)

We are enjoined by this verse to engage in a 'healthy competition' with those whose paths are different from our own: the very differences are themselves part of the foundation for the competition. But the competition is in relation to *good works*, *khayrāt*, and there is no dispute or disagreement about what goodness is: it is immediately recognizable, however different be the processes by which goodness is produced. Dialogue between different religious believers, from this point of view, should generate a healthy competition aimed at 'goodness' which is always and everywhere the same, however different be the religious starting points. This Qur'ānic view of the purpose and goal of dialogue resonates deeply with the stated aims of His Holiness, the Dalai Lama. In his numerous writings and speeches, the Dalai Lama stresses not only that the different religions must remain faithful to their respective traditions, but also that they all, without exception, aim at values which are self-evidently *khayrāt*, so many forms of goodness. Whereas the religions of the world are very different from each other in terms of philosophical doctrines, he writes, 'in terms of training the mind, all major religions are the same. They all have the same potential to transform the human mind. A clear indication of this is that all major religious traditions carry the message of love, compassion, forgiveness, contentment and self-discipline.'[29]

He reinforces the Qur'ānic concept of spiritual 'competition' in his important paper, 'Harmony, Dialogue and Meditation' delivered at the famous 'Gethsemani Encounter', which brought Christian and

---

29. His Holiness, the Dalai Lama, *The Many Ways to Nirvana* (London: Hodder and Stoughton, 2004), p. 5.

Buddhist monks together in dialogue in July, 1996, in Gethsemani, Kentucky. While urging all participants to avoid the temptation to engage in 'advertisement' for one's own tradition, and to guard against a certain kind of unhealthy competition, he maintains nonetheless, 'But I think we should have one kind of constructive competition. The Buddhists should implement what we believe in daily life; and our Christian brothers and sisters should also implement their teachings in daily life.' Implementation of belief is central to the Dalai Lama's vision of the transformative power of 'practice'; it is insofar as 'each side would like to be better practitioners' that the competition between them is constructive and not destructive.[30]

For the Dalai Lama, the very process by which one deepens the practice of one's own tradition illuminates the truth and wisdom of other traditions. For the 'spiritual experience' consequent upon deeper practice enables one 'to see the value of other traditions. Therefore, to promote religious harmony, one should look into one's own tradition seriously, and implement it as much as possible.'[31]

If, by contrast, one restricts oneself to the purely theoretical aspects of one's tradition, then the values which bring human beings together in goodness will be eclipsed by dogmatic coagulations:

> All religions teach a message of love, compassion, sincerity and honesty. Each system seeks in its own way to improve life for us all. Yet if we put too much emphasis on our own philosophy, religion or theory, becoming too attached to it, and try to impose it on other people, the result will be trouble. Basically, all the great teachers, including Gautama Buddha, Jesus Christ, Muhammad and Moses, were motivated by a desire to help their fellow beings. They did not seek to gain anything for themselves, nor to create more trouble in the world.[32]

The Dalai Lama's message on dialogue—on the spiritual dynamics underlying true dialogue—is at once ethically simple and spiritually profound, eminently practicable and philosophically irrefut-

---

30. His Holiness, the Dalai Lama, 'Harmony, Dialogue and Meditation', in D.W. Mitchell, J.Wiseman (eds.) *The Gethsemani Encounter* (New York: Continuum, 1999), p. 49.

31. *The Many Ways to Nirvana*, op. cit., p. 83.

32. His Holiness, the Dalai Lama, *Widening the Circle of Love*, tr. Jeffrey Hopkins (London, Sydney, etc: Rider, 2002), p. 4.

able: if you bring to life, within yourself, the fundamental values of your own religion, you will not only change yourself, you will also change the world:

> Through your kindness towards others, your mind and heart will open to peace. Expanding this inner environment to the larger community around you will bring unity, harmony and cooperation; expanding peace further still to nations and then to the world will bring mutual trust, mutual respect, sincere communication, and fully successful joint efforts to solve the world's problems. All this is possible. But first we must change ourselves. Each one of us is responsible for mankind.[33]

One is reminded here of the verse of the Qur'ān: *Truly God will not change the condition of a people until they change the condition of their own souls* (13:11).

The following passage expresses a compelling picture of the power of the 'dialogical' dynamics that are unleashed by the sincere and ever-deepening *practice* of one's own faith. Those who realized the deepest values of their own faith are referred to by the Dalai Lama, again and again, as 'practitioners', those who engage in the meditative dimensions of their faith alongside the philosophical ones; and it is they who constitute the most effective partners in authentic dialogue:

> It is my belief that if prayer, meditation and contemplation[34] are combined in daily practice, the effect on the practitioner's mind and heart will be all the greater. One of the major aims and purposes of religious practice for the individual is an inner transformation from an undisciplined, untamed, unfocused state of mind toward one that is disciplined, tamed and balanced. A person who has perfected the faculty of single-pointedness will definitely have a greater ability to attain this objective. When meditation becomes an important part of your spiritual life, you are able to bring about this inner transformation in a more effective way. Once this transformation has been achieved, then in following your own spiritual tradition, you will discover that a kind of natu-

---

33. Ibid., pp. 4–5.
34. By the word 'contemplation', the Dalai Lama means, here and in most other contexts read by us, the analytical or philosophical aspects of the tradition.

ral humility will arise in you, allowing you to communicate better with people from other religious traditions and cultural backgrounds. You are in a better position to appreciate the values and preciousness of other traditions because you have seen this value from within your own tradition.[35]

The Dalai Lama then adds a point of inestimable significance for understanding and overcoming the psychology underlying religious fundamentalism; implicit in what he says here is that this kind of fundamentalism or exclusivism arises out of an inability not only to understand other religions, but also an inability to plumb the depth of one's own religion:

> People often experience feelings of exclusivity in their religious beliefs—a feeling that one's own path is the only true path—which can create a sense of apprehension about connecting with others of different faiths. I believe the best way to counter this force is to experience the value of one's own path through a meditative life, which will enable one to see the value and preciousness of other traditions.

It is, then, on the level of practice, both ethical and spiritual, that the Dalai Lama sees the religions of the world coming together in harmony, while maintaining their own specific identities. Strongly opposed to any syncretism, and any attempt to dissolve religious traditions within one universal religion, he instead invites us to participate actively in a vision of universal harmony based on the spirit of wisdom and compassion which emanates from the heart:

> I believe the purpose of all the major religious traditions is not to construct big temples on the outside, but to create temples of goodness and compassion *inside*, in our hearts. Every major religion has the potential to create this. The greater our awareness is regarding the value and effectiveness of other religious traditions, then the deeper will be our respect and reverence toward other religions. This is the proper way for us to promote genuine compassion and a spirit of harmony among the religions of the world.[36]

---

35. *The Good Heart*, op. cit., p. 40.
36. Ibid., pp. 39–40.

In what follows, we intend to make a humble contribution to this inspiring vision of inter-religious harmony by bringing to light the common spiritual and ethical ground underlying the religions of Islam and Buddhism.

Part Two
Oneness: The Highest Common Denominator

Conceiving of the One

Say: He, God, is One
God, the Self-Sufficient Besought of all,[1]
He begets not, nor is begotten,
And there is none like unto Him. (Qur'ān 112:1–4)

There is, monks, an unborn, not become, not made, uncompounded; and were it not, monks, for this unborn, not become, not made, uncompounded, no escape could be shown here for what is born, has become, is made, is compounded.

But because there is, monks, an unborn, not become, not made, uncompounded, therefore an escape can be shown for what is born, has become, is made, is compounded.' (*Udāna*, 80–81)[2]

The juxtaposition of these two scriptural citations shows us the possibility of arguing that the ultimate Reality to which Islam and Buddhism testify is one and the same. One can ask the question: is That which is described as absolutely One in the Qur'ān metaphysically identical to that which is described as 'uncompounded' by the Buddha?

Let us take a look at how this oneness is described in Islam, before comparing it to the 'uncompounded' in Buddhism. The first testimony of Islam, 'No divinity but the one and only Divinity' can be understood to mean not just that there is only one God as opposed to many, but that there is only one absolute, permanent reality—all other realities being relative and ephemeral, totally dependent upon

---

1. This rather wordy translation of the single Arabic word (which is one of the Names of God) *al-Samad* is given by Martin Lings (*The Holy Qur'ān—Translations of Selected Verses*, Royal Aal al-Bayt Institute & The Islamic Texts Society, 2007), p. 200. Lings' translation does full justice to the two fundamental connotations of the name: al-Samad is absolutely self-sufficient, on the one hand, and, for this very reason, is eternally besought by all other beings, on the other. See al-Rāghib al-Isfahānī's classical dictionary of Qur'ānic terms, *Mu'jam mufradāt alfāz al-Qur'ān* (Beirut: Dār al-Fikr, n.d.), p. 294.

2. *Buddhist Texts Through the Ages*, eds. E. Conze, I.B. Horner, D. Snelgrove, A. Waley (Oxford: Bruno Cassirer, 1954), p. 95.

this One reality for its existence: *Everything thereon is passing away* (fān)*; and there subsists* (yabqā) *only the Face of your Lord, Owner of Majesty and Glory* (55:26–27). Thus, this first testimony comes to mean, in metaphysical terms: 'No reality but the one and only Reality'. The false 'gods' of paganism are not just idols made of wood and stone, but also, and more fundamentally, so many erroneous views of reality, so many mistakes on the level of thought. This epistemological mode of affirmation of *tawhīd*, or the oneness of God, together with its corollary, the censure of *shirk*, or idolatry, might be seen to resonate deeply with the following simple statement by the Buddha, which figures in the very first chapter of the *Dhammapada*:

> Those who think the unreal is, and think the Real is not, they shall never reach the Truth, lost in the path of wrong thought.
> But those who know the Real is, and know the unreal is not, they shall indeed reach the Truth, safe on the path of right thought.[3]

This statement echoes the first testimony of Islam, understood metaphysically or epistemologically, rather than simply theologically. It also echoes the verse of the Qur'ān:

> *There is no compulsion in religion. Indeed the right way has been made distinct from error. So whoever rejects* [lit. 'disbelieves': *yakfur*] *the false gods and believes in God, he has truly held tight to the firmest of handles, which can never break* (2:256).

The Unborn

It is possible to discern in the Buddha's saying from the *Udāna* two affirmations of the oneness of ultimate reality, one temporal and the other substantial. At this point we will endeavour to address the temporal aspect, later the substantial aspect, relating to the distinction between compounded and non-compounded, will be addressed. In terms of time, then, the 'unborn' and the 'not become' can be understood to refer to a reality or essence which, being above and beyond the temporal condition, is perforce the origin of that condition; it is from this 'not become' that all becoming originates. This

---

3.*The Dhammapada—The Path of Perfection*, tr. Juan Mascaró (Harmondsworth, UK: Penguin, 1983), I, pp. 11–12.

unnamed degree of reality thus has an explicit resonance with the way in which *Allāh* is described in 112:3, as being unbegotten; and one might discern an implicit relationship with certain dimensions of the divine reality, in particular, 'the First', *al-Awwal*, and 'the Originator', *al-Mubdi*'.

Much more is theologically implied in these qualities of *Allāh* than in the simple reference of the Buddha to what is 'unborn', needless to say, given that in Islamic theology each of the Names designates an attribute of *Allāh*. The sole ontological substance of all the Names is *Allāh*, that which is 'Named' by the Names; each Name thus implies not only the particular quality it designates, but also *Allāh* as such, and thereby all of the other 'ninety-nine' Names of *Allāh*, such as 'the Creator', 'the Judge', 'the Master', 'the Conquerer' etc. Many of these attributes will be alien to the Buddhist conception of what is meant by the 'unborn'. While some Buddhists may feel obliged to deny belief in a divinity possessed of such qualities, others, following the example of the Buddha, will prefer to maintain silence rather than affirming or denying these qualities. Here we see a major, and perhaps unbridgeable, divide between the doctrines of the two faiths on the plane of theology. However, on the plane of metaphysics and even on that of mystical psychology, one might ask whether the Buddha's silences can be interpreted positively, in the light of his clear affirmation of the Absolute as that which is 'unborn, not become, not made, uncompounded'; if so, then his 'non-theism' will not be seen as negating the Essence of the Absolute which transcends all attributes, but rather, as methodically ignoring every attribute that can be predicated of this Absolute— ignoring that is, the Personal divinity, for the sake of an exclusive focus on the supra-Personal Essence. If, by contrast, one interprets his silences negatively, that is, as if they implied a negation of the things about which he remained silent, then one will be making his 'non-theism' into an 'atheism', a denial both of the Personal divinity and of the supra-Personal Essence—the Essence implied by the Personal divinity, and without which the Personal divinity is nothing.

Nobody can deny that the Buddha's doctrine is non-theistic: there is no Personal divinity playing the role of Creator, Revealer, Judge in Buddhism. But to assert that the Buddha's doctrine is 'atheistic' would be to attribute to him an explicit denial and negation of the Absolute—which one does not find anywhere in his teachings. The citation we have given above from the Udāna, 80–81, together with several other verses from the Pali canon which one could cite, makes it clear that the Buddha did indeed conceive of the Absolute, and that this Absolute is affirmed as the ultimate Reality, to which one must 'escape'. There is a conception—and therefore an affirmation—of this Reality, however 'minimalist' such a conception is as compared to the more detailed theological conception found in Islam. The fact that there is a conception and affirmation of the Absolute makes it difficult to qualify the Buddhist doctrine as atheistic.

Mention was made of mystical psychology above. This is connected with the use of the word 'escape' in *Udāna* 80–81. It will be recalled that *Nirvāna* as described by the Buddha was framed entirely in terms of an escape from bondage into supreme security:

- unborn supreme security from bondage
- unageing supreme security from bondage
- unailing supreme security from bondage
- deathless supreme security from bondage
- sorrowless supreme security from bondage
- undefiled supreme security from bondage[4]

The whole purpose of presenting the reality of the uncompounded—of the unageing, unailing, deathless, sorrowless and the undefiled—is to escape from what is compounded, subject to old age, death, sorrow and defilement. In other words, the Buddha was not primarily concerned with describing, in theological mode, the various attributes of the Absolute, but rather with stressing the imperative need of escaping to the Absolute; escaping, that is, from the painful illusions of the relative—the compounded—to the blissful reality of the Absolute, which is Nirvāna. Here we feel a resonance with such verses in the Qur'ān as the following: *...when the earth, vast as it is, became narrow for them, and their own souls became narrow for them, such that they knew that there is no refuge from God except in Him* (9:118); *... so escape unto God* (51:50).

From the point of view of these verses, what matters is the urgency of fleeing from the world of sin and suffering to the only refuge, that of the Absolute. In a situation of dire urgency, we do not ask for subtle definitions of what it is that will save us. It is this urgency which Buddhist teachings directly address, it is this urgency which determines the modalities and the language of the Buddha's message. It is this urgency which provides one answer to the ques-

---

4. *The Middle Length Discourses*, op. cit., 26:18, pp. 259–260.

tion which plagues Muslim-Buddhist dialogue: why, Muslims ask, do the Buddhists deny the existence of a Creator? We would argue, first, that such a denial goes much further than the Buddha himself went; and secondly, that if one takes into account the context of the Buddha's teachings, the reason why he chose not to speak of such a Creator-God becomes more intelligible. First, the fact that the Buddha refused, on the whole, to speak of the process by which the 'compounded' elements come together in the world that we see around us does not imply the necessity of denying the objective existence of a dimension of the Absolute which can be called 'the Creator'. The Buddha's silence was part of his 'mystical rhetoric', one might say: the dialectical stress of his teachings was on escaping from the suffering attendant upon the compounded world, rather than on understanding the cosmological process by which one becomes enslaved by that compounded world. Let us look at this mystical rhetoric a little more closely.

Buddhist Dialectics

This rhetorical or dialectical mode of teaching needs to be understood by reference to the specific nature of the environment in which the Buddha's message was promulgated. As we saw earlier, the Qur'ān tells us: *And We never sent a messenger save with the language of his people, so that he might make it clear to them* (14:4). The 'language' of the Buddha's people must be understood in the wider sense of the religious and cultural context of India in his time. This context was defined by a largely pharisaical and formalistic Brahmanical culture, wherein one of the chief obstacles to effective salvation was a preoccupation with the putatively 'eternal' nature of the soul. The transcendence of the Absolute Self (*Paramātman*) was lost sight of amid the formulaic, one-sided assertions of the immanence of the Absolute Self in the relative self (*jīvātman*), the result being a diminution of a sense of the utter otherness of the Absolute Self vis-à-vis the relativity of the human self. Immanence had trumped transcendence; the immortality of the soul was confused with the eternity of the Absolute. If salvation had become reduced by the 'eternalists' to a blithe self-projection into eternity, it was rejected altogether by the 'annihilationists' as a piece of wishful thinking by those who could not accept the grim reality of nothingness: nothing of the soul exists after death, according to these annihilationists, it dies with the body.[5]

As the following citation from a Chinese text from the Middle Way school[6] tells us, it is not a question of asserting one position to the exclusion of the other, but rather seeking to discover a 'middle way' between the two:

> Only seeing that all are empty without seeing the non-empty side — this cannot be called Middle Way. Only seeing that all have no self without also seeing the self — this cannot be called Middle Way.[7]

Nāgārjūna explains the fundamental distinction between the two different planes of reality and the truths proportioned thereto, a distinction which helps us to decipher the Buddha's paradoxical, apparently contradictory, statements about the soul, and indeed about Reality: 'The teaching of the doctrine by the Buddhas is based upon two truths: truth relating to worldly convention and truth in terms of ultimate fruit.'[8] It is on the level of conventional truth (*samvrti-satyam*) that one can assert the relative reality of the individual soul, and it is likewise on this level of reality that one can situate the processes of dependent origination, clinging, delusion and suffering. However, completely transcending this level of explanation, and the world (*loka*) proportioned to it, is the truth or reality pertaining to 'ultimate fruit' (*paramārtha*). On the level of ultimate Reality—which is seen only upon enlightenment, and, prior to enlightenment, glimpsed through intuitions—the individual soul is itself perceived as an illusion, and all that pertains to the world within which the soul apparently exists is illusory. That which is permanent is alone real.

However, this does not prevent suffering from being what it is for

---

5. For a detailed presentation of the Buddha's religious environment and the views of the 'eternalists' (*sassata-ditthiyo*) and annihilationists' (*uccheda-ditthiyo*), see K.N. Jayatilleke, *Early Buddhist Theory of Knowledge* (London: George Allen & Unwin, 1963), pp. 21–168; and for a concise summary of the speculative views not held by the Buddha, see the dialogue between the Buddha and the wanderer Vacchagotta in Sutta 72 (*Aggivacchagotta*) of *The Middle Length Discourses*, op. cit., pp. 590–594.

6. *Mādhyamika*, the school founded by Nāgārjūna, referred to in the introduction.

7. *Taisho shinshū daizokyo* 12, 374: 523b, cited by Youru Wang in *Linguistic Strategies in Daoist Zhuangzi and Chan Buddhism* (London & New York: RoutledgeCurzon, 2003), p. 61.

8. From his *Mūlamadhyamakakārikā*, 24:8, cited by David Kalupahana, *Nāgārjūna—The Philosophy of the Middle Way*, op. cit., p. 331.

the soul plunged in illusion, the soul which is still held in bondage to the relative world of name and form (*nama-rupa*). The suffering is real enough, but the domain within which suffering exists is itself ultimately unreal: the impermanence of the world (*anicca*) and the unreality of the soul (*anattā*) are thus mutually empowering teachings which lead to the cessation of suffering through grasping not just the nature of the Void, but also, the bliss of Nirvana inherent in that Void.

Continuing with the concept of the Middle Way, and showing how this later school of thought is rooted in the earliest scriptures, the following discourse of the Buddha to Kaccāyana (*Kaccāyanagotta-Sutta*) should be noted:

> 'Everything exists'—this, Kaccāyana, is one extreme. 'Everything does not exist'—this, Kaccāyana, is the second extreme. Kaccāyana, without approaching either extreme, the Tathāgata[9] teaches you a doctrine by the middle.

The teaching continues with a demonstration that ignorance is at the root of all suffering: from ignorance arises a chain of causality, each factor generating its inevitable consequence: dispositions, consciousness, psycho-physical personality, senses, contact, feeling, craving, grasping, becoming, birth, old age and death, grief, lamentation, suffering, dejection and despair. 'Thus arises this entire mass of suffering. However, from the utter fading away and ceasing of ignorance, there is a ceasing of dispositions', and the whole chain of interdependent causality is brought to an end: 'And thus there is the ceasing of the entire mass of suffering.'[10]

Ignorance is here identified with its ultimate consequence, suffering; salvation from suffering is thus achieved through knowledge. If the issue of salvation had become smothered by wrongly posed alternatives in the Buddha's time, the question of the creation and origination of the cosmos had likewise become more a source of speculative distraction than constructive elucidation. This point is well made in the following verses, which shed considerable light on the whole dialectical purpose and intent of the Buddhist teaching as a 'skilful means' (*upāya-kauśala*) by which people are oriented to the imperative of salvation:

---

9. This term means both 'one thus gone,' and at the same time 'one thus come'. See the introduction for discussion.

10. *Kaccāyanagotta-Sutta* in *Samutta-nikāya*, 2.17; cited by David J. Kalupahana, *Nāgārjūna—The Philosophy of the Middle Way*, op. cit., pp. 10–11.

Suppose, Mālunkyaputta, a man were pierced with an arrow well steeped in poison, and his close friends and relatives were to summon a physician, a surgeon. Then suppose the man says, I will not have this arrow pulled out until I know, of the man by whom I was pierced, both his name and clan, and whether he be tall or short or of middle stature: till I know him whether he be a black man or dark or sallow-skinned: whether he be from such and such a village or suburb or town. I will not have the arrow pulled out until I know of the bow by which I was pierced, whether it was a long-bow or a cross-bow …' This questioning continues, in regard to all sorts of details about the arrow. 'Well, Mālunkyaputta, that man would die, but still the matter would not be found out by him.[11]

This one-pointed focus on the need to overcome ignorance, delusion and suffering meant that the Buddha refused to answer questions which would only further entrench the ignorance he was so keen to dispel. What he was silent about, however, he did not deny.

Like all the 'gods' or divine attributes in the Hindu culture of the Buddha's time, Brahmā the Creator (masculine gender, as distinct from Brahma, neuter, referring to the Absolute) had become reified as a concept. The solidarity between an individual soul, deemed eternal, and the gods, also relativities endowed with eternity, needed to be sundered. Hence the doctrine of 'no soul' went hand in hand with that of 'impermanence' on all levels, human and divine. The 'denial of the soul' was in fact a denial that the soul was eternal, and this most imperative of all messages was rendered all the more effective if it were combined with the idea that even the 'gods', or divine attributes, were not eternal. Included in the category of the 'gods' was that of the Creator, Brahmā, who, while not being denied outright, is perceived as one among other relativities. Attention to creation translated into distraction from the eternal; for this reason, Buddhism remains largely silent about the source of creation, and keeps our attention riveted to the requirements of salvation from the suffering attendant upon attachment to the 'created' world.

This point emerges with particular clarity in the immensely influential text in the Mahayana tradition, *The Flower Ornament*

---

11. *Majjhima Nikāya* I, 63; cited in *Some Sayings*, op. cit., p. 305.

36

Scripture (*Avatamsaka Sutra*, called *Huayan* in Chinese), briefly referred to earlier.[12] Let us consider first the following verses:

> All things have no provenance and no one can create them:
> There is nowhere whence they are born
> They cannot be discriminated.
> All things have no provenance,
> Therefore they have no birth;
> Because there is no birth,
> Neither can extinction be found.
> All things are birthless
> And have no extinction either;
> Those who understand in this way
> Will see the Buddha.[13]

The fact that these statements on the beginningless nature of things—and thus the absence of a Creator thereof—are intended more as mystical pedagogy than rational theology, or a denial of the existence of the Creator, is indicated, among other things, by the following verses, which focus attention on the fact that wisdom or enlightenment is the eternally present reality, which has never not been; the absence of wisdom is what is illusory, and the very idea that it could have once been non-existent, and is then 'born' entrenches the mind in the illusions of temporal succession, keeping it remote from the reality of eternity:

> There's nothing the Buddha knows not,
> Therefore he's inconceivable.
> Never from lack of wisdom
> Has wisdom ever been born.[14]

A wisdom that could emerge into existence after having been non-existent cannot be authentic wisdom, which is one with the nature of the Absolute. This wisdom itself renders the Buddha 'inconceivable'—or renders 'it', the state of 'the awakened one' inconceiv-

---

12. This text is also known as 'the major Scripture of Inconceivable Liberation', as the translator, Thomas Cleary, notes, adding 'it is perhaps the richest and most grandiose of all Buddhist scriptures, held in high esteem by all schools of Buddhism that are concerned with universal liberation.' *The Flower Ornament Scripture*, op. cit., p. 1.

13. Ibid., p. 445. As will be made clearer below, 'the Buddha' is identified with the enlightened state and not just the human being; and it is also identified with the ultimate Reality, as the objective content of the enlightened state.

14. Ibid., p. 447.

able: were it conceivable, it would be an object known, as opposed to the knowing subject. This echoes the Qur'ānic teaching: *Vision comprehends Him not, but He comprehends all vision. He is the Subtle, the Aware* (6:103). Such inconceivable knowledge cannot be attained by means of any conception; it can only be realized through enlightenment, and the only purpose of all conceptions, all words, is to negate the pretensions of conceptual thought, and pave the way for an intuition of That which goes beyond all formal thought, being their ontological infrastructure—the infinite being from which all thought and existence is derived. Such 'wisdom' has never been 'born' from anything which could be described as an absence of wisdom: 'never from lack of wisdom has wisdom ever been born'. To drive home the liberating power of this truth, any speculative foray into the domain of what has 'been born', and which, by that token might possibly become born—and thus also must perish—is nothing but a distraction from the one thing needful: enlightenment.

There is, then, no absolute denial of a Creator. But the idea of a Creator—within the overall context of the Buddhist *upāya*, dominated as it is by the imperative of escape from the conditioned to the unconditioned—is liable to detract from the intensity of concentration required for taking the leap from the present moment into eternity. For this leap requires one to utterly ignore the temporal notions of past and future, which do not exist, it is only ever the present moment which is real. This idea is expressed in one verse by the simple negation that the Buddhas were ever really born or died: 'The Buddhas do not come forth into the world, and they have no extinction'. Commenting on this, Thomas Cleary writes, 'all Buddhas attain great enlightenment by the timeless essence. Instantly seeing the Way, views of past and present end, "new" and "old" do not exist at all—one attains the same enlightenment as countless Buddhas of the past, and also becomes Buddha at the same time as the Buddhas of countless ages of the future, by personally witnessing the timelessness of the past, present, and future. Because there is no time, there is no coming or going.' [15] This serves also as a comment on the following verses of the *Avatamsaka Sutra:*

Just as the future
Has not the marks of the past,
So also do all things
Not have any marks at all.

15. Ibid., p. 51.

Just as the signs of birth and death
Are all unreal
So also are all things
Void of intrinsic nature.
Nirvana cannot be grasped,
But when it is spoken of there are two kinds,
So it is of all things:
When discriminated, they are different.
Just as based on something counted
There exists a way of counting.
Their nature is nonexistent:
Thus are phenomena perfectly known.
It's like the method of counting,
Adding one, up to infinity;
The numbers have no substantial nature:
They are distinguished due to intellect.[16]

To speak of the past—and a fortiori, any 'creator' or originator of what was 'in the beginning'—is to engage in something akin to 'the method of counting'. One can add one continuously to each number in the series, and never come to an end; one will never, through counting, realize that 'numbers have no substantial nature'. Here, 'numbers' stand for all phenomena, which stand apart from the unitive Reality: to engage in thought with the origin of phenomena is to engage with those phenomena, from this point of view: what the Buddhist logic of enlightenment calls for, on the contrary, is the radical transcendence of phenomena, which in turn requires one to ignore completely the process by which phenomena came into being, whence the apparent denial of the Creator.

* * *

The 'non-theism' of Buddhism not only upholds what Muslims refer to as the Oneness of God; it can also deepen the Muslim's appreciation of the utter transcendence of God, helping to show that the divine Essence radically negates all relativity, and that all of our conceptions of that Essence are perforce mediated through veils of our own subjective construction. God can indeed be described according to the images, qualities and allusions given in the Revelation, but between all of these descriptions and the true reality of God there is still no common measure. *They measure God not according to His true*

---

16. Ibid., p. 448.

measure (6:91). No human conception of God—even if fashioned by ideas received through Revelation—can be identified with the transcendent reality of the divine Essence; it cannot overcome the incommensurability separating the relative from the Absolute.

The Muslim conception of the Essence of God, transcending all Names and Qualities, will be recognizable to Buddhists as an allusion to that ineffable reality which 'no words or speech can reach'.[17] This is a refrain in the Qur'ān: 'Glorified be God above what they describe' (*subhāna'Llāhi 'ammā yasifūn*) is a constant refrain in the Qur'ān; it refers in the first instance to the false descriptions of God, or false ascriptions of divinity to idols; but it also alludes to this fundamental theological principle of Islam: the Essence of God is utterly indefinable, above and beyond the divine Qualities manifesting It, indeed, infinitely surpassing any conceivable 'thing': *There is nothing like Him* (42:11).

Whereas the Qur'ān is full of descriptions of God's actions and attributes—thus expressing a cataphatic or even an anthropomorphic conception of God, so far removed from the Buddhist conception of an impersonal ultimate reality—one can nonetheless find both in the Qur'ān and the sayings of the Prophet, certain crucial openings to an apprehension of the Essence of God which utterly transcends all categories of human language, cognition, and conception, including all those which are fashioned by the very descriptions of God's acts and attributes given in His own revelation. Buddhist apophatic philosophy can thus be read as an elaboration upon the *nafy*, the negation, of the first testimony of Islam: *lā ilāha*, 'no divinity'. The *ithbāt*, or affirmation, *illa'Llāh*, 'except the Divinity', can be read in this context as the intuition of an ineffable Reality which arises in the very measure that all false conceptions of reality have been eliminated. It is that Reality which is not susceptible to negation, and that to which the Muslim mystics testify as being the content of their ultimate realization: *al-fanā'*, extinction of the self (false reality/divinity), gives way to *al-baqā'*, subsistence of the Self (true Reality/Divinity). Mystic experience thus mirrors the two elements, the *nafy* and the *ithbāt*, of the first testimony of Islam.

Shūnya and Shahāda

It is possible to argue that the implication of the doctrine of the 'Void' (*Shūnya*) or 'Extinction' (*Nirvāna*) is akin to the highest meaning of

---

17. Ibid., p. 291.

the *nafy* of the *Shahāda*. If the 'non-theism' of Buddhism can be understood as a commentary on the *nafy* of the first testimony of Islam, 'no divinity', then the *ithbāt* of the first testimony can be understood within Buddhism as pertaining to the ultimate, supra-personal Essence of God. That Absolute, alone, is ultimately real, the Buddhist would assert, and one can only refer to it in terms that negate any hint of relativity, thus, in apophatic terms: It is the 'un-born', the 'uncompound', the 'Void'—for It is de-void of all relativity, all otherness, all conditionality. Here we are confronted by the 'substantial' aspect of the text cited above, *Udāna*, 80–81. Being devoid of everything but itself, this Absolute, alone, is 'simple'[18] (non-compound), 'purely itself', thus at one with the absolute purity of *ikhlās*, a key Islamic term which means 'purification' as well as 'sincerity', and is one of the titles of *Sūra* 112 cited above. Sincerity flows forth in the measure that one's conception of God is 'purified' of any stain of multiplicity; God's pure oneness must be mirrored in the purity of our conception of that oneness, and this gives rise to sincerity. God's oneness, alone, is totally and purely Itself, with no hint of otherness sullying Its nature and rendering it compound; that which is absolutely non-compound, purely 'itself' and nothing but itself, cannot but be absolutely one. This is what is strictly implied by the term 'uncompounded' (*asamskrta*) in verses 80–81 of the *Udāna*, cited above.

When it is stated that all other things are compounded, this means that every single thing in existence is a mixture of different elements, it has no innate, abiding essence of its own. In Islamic terms, all things other than God are likewise seen to be composed of different elements; nothing but God is utterly one, purely itself. Pure oneness transcends all multiplicity.

However, that oneness is manifested, symbolically, on the level of form. This is what is called *Shunyamurti* in Buddhism, literally: the manifestation of the Void. The Void as such cannot be manifested without ceasing to be the Void, but it can be symbolically expressed. One might also see the very name of God in Islam, *Allāh*, as just such a manifestation of the Void, being a symbolic designation of That which is beyond all possible conception and form. As we shall see below, the transcendent reality of God is strictly inaccessible

---

18. 'Simple' translates the Arabic *basīt*, as opposed to *murakkab* 'compounded'. Let us recall that the English word 'simple' is derived from the root 'sim', related to 'same', thus to identity, unity.

in its Essence. One of the ways in which It is glorified is precisely by declaring its transcendent incomparability (*tanzīh*). However, the same reality is also glorified in its manifestation on the level of form, in the name *Allāh*—and all other Names of God—which reflect that reality within language and thought. Thus, one glorifies God—qua Essence—as in the refrain '*Glorified be God above what they describe*'; but one also glorifies God's 'Name': '*Glorify the Name of thy Lord, Most High*'. The Name of that which is beyond all words and thought thus becomes something akin to a 'manifestation of the Void'. The deliverance offered by this saving manifestation, by means of invocation, will be addressed below, in the section entitled 'Remembrance of God'.

Light of Transcendence

The Buddhist perspective can be seen to reinforce the Muslim message of divine transcendence. It reminds Muslims of the need to be aware of the existence of the conceptual veils through which we perforce view the divine Sun, whose light is so bright that it blinds the conceptual 'eye' of one who presumes to look upon it. This is expressed most precisely in the following saying of the Prophet: 'God has seventy thousand veils of light and darkness; were He to remove them, the glories of His Countenance would consume all those who looked upon Him.' [19] The Qur'ān, similarly, alludes to the unapproachability of the divine Essence: *God warns you to beware of His Self* (3:28, repeated at 3:30). One can cogitate or meditate (engage in *fikr/tafakkur*) only upon the qualities of God, and not upon His Essence. As al-Rāghib al-Isfahānī, a major lexicographer of the Qur'ān, writes in his explanation of the Qur'ānic concept of *fikr*: 'Meditation is only possible in regard to that which can assume a conceptual form (*sūra*) in one's heart. Thus we have the following saying [of the Prophet]: Meditate upon the bounties of God but not

---

19. *Sahīh Muslim*, Book of *Īmān*, 293. There is a deeper mystical meaning to the destruction wrought by the vision of God. This relates to the very heart of sanctity or *walāya* in Islam, understood metaphysically. The saint is the one who has indeed been blessed with the vision of God, and has been rendered 'extinct' in the very same sense as in the Buddhist *nirvana*, which means, precisely, 'extinction'. Though being commented upon chiefly by the Sufis, this aspect of the supreme realisation is also alluded to in several Qur'ānic verses and prophetic sayings. Suffice it here to refer to one Qur'ānic verse which hints at this mystery: 'If you claim to be saints of God (*awliyā' Allāh*), favoured above others, then long for death, if you are sincere.' (62:6)

on God [Himself, His Essence] for God is above and beyond all possibility of being described in terms of any form (*sūra*).' [20]

The basic idea expressed in this saying of the Prophet has been transmitted in various forms:[21] one can meditate on 'all things', on the 'qualities' of God, but not on His Essence, to which no powers of conception have any access. This means that in Islamic terms, the ultimate Reality is utterly inconceivable; that which is conceivable cannot be the ultimate Reality. The capacity to conceive of this distinction between the conceivable and the inconceivable lies, paradoxically, at the very heart of the *Shahāda*, understood metaphysically rather than just theologically: we must be aware that the initial conception we have of the one and only Reality is but a starting point, not a conclusion; this conception is an initiation into a spiritual mystery, not the consummation of a chain of mental constructs; it initiates one into a transformative movement towards the Ineffable, of which the mind can glimpse but a shadow. The Islamic view of the utter transcendence of God's Essence, the belief that It surpasses all possible modes of formal conception, thus shows that there are no grounds for erecting simplistic reified conceptions of God in Islam; it also helps the Buddhist to see that, at the very summit of Islamic metaphysics, and even, at a stretch, Islamic theology, there is an application of the first *Shahāda* which resonates deeply with the Buddhist insistence on the Void, *Shūnya*, being beyond *namarūpa* (name/form), and by that very token, beyond all conceivability. Both traditions would appear to be able to agree on the following paraphrase of the *Shahāda*: 'no conceivable form: only the inconceivable Essence'.

Al-Samad and *Dharma*

The Islamic distinction between the oneness of God's Essence and the multiplicity of creation evokes the Buddhist distinction between the oneness of the uncompounded and the multiplicity of the compounded. This conceptual similarity is further reinforced by the meaning of the term *Samad*: in addition to being positively described as that which is eternally self-sufficient, and that which is sought by all else, it is also apophatically referred to as 'that which

---

20. *Mu'jam mufradāt*, op. cit., p. 398.

21. Jalāl al-Dīn al-Suyūtī cites 5 variations on this saying in his compilation of prophetic sayings, *al-Jāmi' al-Saghīr* (Beirut: Dar al-Ma'rifa, 1972), vol. 3, pp. 262–263.

is not empty or hollow' (*ajwaf*).[22] This immediately brings to mind the fundamental Buddhist belief that the *Dharma*, as such, is alone 'full', all other *dharmas* are 'empty', empty that is, of 'self being' (*svabhāva*). Indeed, one of the most fundamental propositions common to all schools of Mahayana Buddhism is the 'emptiness' of all specific '*dharmas*': 'selfless are all *dharmas*, they have not the character of living beings, they are without a soul, without a personality.'[23]

In other words, as applied to any existent entity, the word '*dharma*' implies an emptiness deprived of suchness, whereas the *Dharma* as such is absolute Suchness. Relative *dharmas* cannot sustain themselves; they depend entirely for their existence on a range of other *dharmas*, nothing in existence being free from dependence upon an indefinite series of factors, all of which are interdependent, and at the same time totally dependent upon the *Dharma* as such, which alone is 'full' of Itself. The *Dharma* has no 'hollowness' or emptiness within it,[24] but rather, just as in the case of *al-Samad*, it is that to which all 'empty' things resort in order to be filled with being, a being which, however, never ceases to be that of the Absolute; it does not become a property or defining quality of the relative things, which are all fatally marked by impermanence and unreality, even while they are endowed with existence.

In Buddhist texts the *Dharma* is stressed as the ultimate Essence of all things or their ultimate Suchness (*tathatā*); but to avoid any possible reification of this Essence, either in thought or in language, the Suchness is in turn identified with the Void (*Shūnya*). What separates the Suchness per se from such and such a conception one might have of It is as vast as that which separates the experience of enlightenment from the mere notion of enlightenment. Radical incommensurability is always maintained as between the *Dharma*/Void/Suchness and any conceptions one may have thereof.

The Void, therefore, is 'empty' only from the point of view of the false plenitude of the world, and of the reifying tendencies of human thought and language. In itself, it is infinite plenitude; in reality,

22. *Mu'jam mufradāt*, op. cit., p. 94.

23. *Diamond Sutra*, cited in E.Conze, *Buddhist Wisdom Books* (London: George Allen & Unwin, 1958), p. 59.

24. The Sanskrit root of this word is *dhri*, 'to hold'. It thus refers to anything which is '*held* to be real', from teachings and precepts to ultimate reality. See Red Pine, *The Zen Teaching of Bodhidharma* (New York: North Point Press, 1987), p. 116, n.6.

it is the world, together with all its reified ramifications in thought, that is empty. The apophatic definition of the Void can thus be seen not as being more indicative of the reality of the *Dharma* than are the cataphatic descriptions thereof: the dialectical stress is on the transcendence of the *Dharma* vis-à-vis both positive and negative designations of its reality. The discourse on the Void appears to be aimed at generating receptivity to a mystical state rather than generating logical conclusions from a series of premises. One is invited to grasp, in a moment of supra-rational intuition, the impossibility of attaining an adequate representation of the *Dharma* in terms of any negative/positive polarity, whether conceptual or linguistic. This very intuition enhances, in turn, receptivity to the sole means of 'understanding' the *Dharma*. The only way in which the *Dharma* can be understood is if it be realized, in the sense of 'made real', spiritually and mystically. Such a realization strictly presupposes transcending the empirical self and all the relative faculties of perception and cognition appended to that self. As will be seen below, such an approach to realization resonates deeply with the mystical tradition in Islam.

In some Buddhist texts it seems that the very emptiness of things constitutes their 'suchness',[25] and it is this emptiness/suchness which relates the thing to the 'suchness' of the *Dharma*, as it were by inverse analogy. It would appear that the *Dharma* is indeed the true suchness of all things, but these 'things' have no access to this suchness except through the negation of their own specificity, compounded as they are of various aggregates arising in mutually dependent chains of causality (*pratītyasamutpāda*)—all of which are empty. So, in spiritual terms, the negation of this emptiness implies being empty of emptiness, and this double negation is the sole means of realizing, in supra-conceptual mode, the Suchness of *Tathatā*.

The *Dharma* is therefore absolute plenitude in its own suchness; but from the point of view of the apparent 'suchness' of the world, it appears to be 'empty': it is empty of all the illusory suchness of things, so, being empty of emptiness, it is infinite plenitude. Thus, when applied to Absolute reality, the same term, '*dharma*', implies an emptiness which is not only absolute plenitude, it also as it were 'fills' the emptiness of all other *dharmas*, which are thereby

25. 'What is empty is Buddha-nature (*Buddhadhātu*)', according to the *Mahāparinirvāna Sūtra*. Cited in ibid., p. 60.

re-endowed with reality. It is for this reason that we find as one of the most definitive Mahayana formulae: '*Samsara* is *Nirvana*; *Nirvana* is *Samsara*'. Relativity is first stripped of its separative existence, and then re-endowed with reality, the sole reality of *Nirvana*—which can be understood as the beatific state proper to the supreme noncompounded Reality. In Islamic terms, one might say: first comes the *nafy*, no divinity/reality; then the *ithbāt*: except the one Divinity/Reality. If we translate the word '*dharma*' as 'essence', and apply it to the formula of the first *shahāda*, we have the following: 'no *dharma*/essence but the *Dharma*/Essence'. The conceptual convergence at this level of *tawhīd*—literally 'affirming, declaring or realizing oneness'—is evident.

We could also say, applying this formula to the Buddha himself: 'no buddha but the *Buddhadhātu*', this latter term referring to the 'Buddha-nature' which is immanent in all things. This immanent Buddha-hood transcends the person of the Buddha, and this is demonstrated by the fact that *Buddhadhātu* is coterminous with *Dharmadhātu*, Dharma-nature, and also with *Tathāgatagarbha*, literally: the 'womb' of the *Tathāgata*, the 'one thus gone'[26]: 'There is neither arising nor perishing within the *Tathāgatabarbha*. It is free from conceptual knowledge and views. Like the nature of *Dharmadhatu*, which is ultimate, wholly complete, and pervades all ten directions ....'[27]

God's Face

In the Qur'ān, God's 'Face' (*wajh*) is identified with the eternal and ubiquitous nature of the divine Reality. In the verses cited above, 55:26–27, we were told that everything in existence is passing away except the 'Face' of God. In another verse we are told: *Everywhere you turn, there is the Face of God* (2:115). In the following verse, the mystery of this 'Face' deepens, and brings home the extent of its correspondence with the Buddhist conception of the *Dharma*: *Every thing is perishing (hālik) except His Face.* (28:88) The Face in question is clearly that of God, but the pronoun 'His' can also be

---

26. One notes here the similarity with the Islamic name of God, *al-Rahmān*, which is derived from the word *Rahim*, meaning womb. See the discussion of *rahma* as all-embracing compassionate love below.

27. From the *Sūtra of Complete Enlightenment* (tr. Ven. Guo-gu Bhikshu) in Master Sheng-yen, *Complete Enlightenment*, part 9, volume 7 (New York: Dharma Drum, 1997), pp. 17–18.

read as pertaining to each 'thing', so that the meaning becomes: every thing is perishing except *its* Face—the Face of that thing. One of the greatest spiritual authorities of Islam, Imam al-Ghazālī (d.1111), comments on this verse as follows: '[It is] not that each thing is perishing at one time or at other times, but that it is perishing from eternity without beginning to eternity without end. It can only be so conceived since, when the essence of anything other than Him is considered in respect of its own essence, it is sheer nonexistence. But when it is viewed in respect of the "face" to which existence flows forth from the First, the Real, then it is seen as existing not in itself but through the face turned to its giver of existence. Hence the only existent is the Face of God. Each thing has two faces: a face toward itself, and a face toward its Lord. Viewed in terms of the face of itself, it is nonexistent; but viewed in terms of the Face of God, it exists. Hence nothing exists but God and His Face.'[28]

With the help of this commentary, we can understand more clearly what is meant by the following verse: *He is the First and the Last, the Outward and the Inward* (57:3). The absolute unity of God is thus both utterly transcendent and inescapably immanent. Not only is the divine Reality within all things as the 'Inward' (*al-Bātin*), it is also the true reality, the 'face' or 'essence' of all empirical phenomena, as the 'Outward', (*al-Zāhir*). It is for this reason that we can look nowhere in existence without being confronted by 'the Face of God'. This rigorous view of the oneness of divine reality rejoins the subtlety of the Mahayana Buddhist view of the ultimate unity of *Samsara* and *Nirvana*. In the words of Milarepa, the greatest poet-saint of Tibet:[29] 'Try to understand that *Nirvana* and *Samsara* are not two ... The core of the View lies in non-duality'.[30] *Samsara*, or relativity, is but the outward, visible 'face' of Nirvana: the outward and the inward, alike, are expressions of the One which transcends the very distinction between these two dimensions. It is only from what Nāgārjūna calls the view of 'conventional reality' (*samvrti-satyam*) that one can distinguish between different 'di-

28. *Al-Ghazālī—The Niche of Lights*, tr. David Buchman (Provo, Utah: Brigham Young University Press, 1998), pp. 16–17. Translation slightly modified: the word *yalī* is better translated as 'turned to' rather than Buchman's 'adjacent to', in the phrase: 'through the face turned to its giver of existence.'

29. See the classic biography by W.Y. Evans-Wentz, *Tibet's Great Yogī Milarepa* (London: Humphrey Milford, 1928).

30. *The Hundred Thousand Songs of Milarepa*, tr. Garma C.C. Chang (Boston & Shaftsbury: Shambhala, 1989), vol. 2, pp. 404, 405.

mensions' whether of space or of time. From the point of view of 'ultimate fruit' (*paramārtha*), however, the Absolute is infinite and eternal, comprising all possible dimensions of space and time, and by that very token not susceptible of location within either space or time. The Qur'ānic notion of the inescapability of the 'face' of God, its immanence in all that exists, is mirrored in the Buddhist idea of a Buddha being present in all things. To cite Milarepa again:

> The Matrix of Buddhahood permeates all sentient beings.
> All beings are therefore Buddhas in themselves.
> Yet they are veiled by temporal defilements;
> Once the defilements are cleansed,
> Then will they be Buddhas.[31]

Milarepa also refers to the 'face' which becomes visible when the substance of one's own consciousness—one's own 'face' of reality— is grasped as identical to the substance of all other beings. In Qur'ānic terms, the Face of God becomes visible through all things, whose true being, or 'face', is not their own, but that of God:

> By realizing that all forms are self-awareness,
> I have beheld my consort's face—the true Mind within.
> So none of the sentient beings in the Three Great Worlds
> Eludes the embrace of this great Thatness.[32]

The 'emptiness' of all *dharmas* might now be seen as the negative prelude to the affirmation of the suchness of the one and only *Dharma*; all particular 'faces' are subsumed within the one and only Face of God. Of particular importance in this connection is the comment of al-Ghazālī: 'when the essence of anything other than Him is considered in respect of its own essence, it is sheer nonexistence'. One need only replace the word 'essence' with '*dharma*', and nonexistence with 'emptiness' and we are confronted with what sounds like a perfectly Buddhist formulation. The doctrine of the emptiness or unreality of all *dharmas*, in turn, leads directly to the Islamic principle of *tawhīd*, as the following verses from the *Satasāhasrika* show:

> From the first thought of enlightenment onwards, a Bo-
> dhisattva should train himself in the conviction that all

31. Ibid., vol. 2, p. 391.
32. Ibid., vol. 2, p. 370.

*dharma*s are baseless. While he practices the six perfections he should not take anything as a basis[33] … Where there is duality, there is a basis. Where there is non-duality there is lack of basis.

Subhuti: How do duality and non-duality come about?

The Lord: Where there is eye and forms, ear and sounds, [etc., to:] where there is mind and *dharmas*, where there is enlightenment and the enlightened, that is duality. Where there is no eye and forms, no ear and sounds, [etc., to:] no mind and *dharmas*, no enlightenment and the enlightened, that is non-duality.[34]

It may seem strange at first sight that even 'the enlightened' are included in the sphere of duality. The reason is that, from this point of view of pure enlightenment, nothing but that quality of pure consciousness exists; if one speaks of the consciousness that belongs or pertains to an individual, then there is, unavoidably, a duality: the one who is conscious, and the content of his consciousness. This is precisely what is taught in the mystical Islamic doctrine of *fanā'*.

Fanā' and Non-duality

The discerning of a subtle dualism in the consciousness of one who is enlightened, or on the path to enlightenment, finds expression in the text of al-Ghazālī cited earlier. In the following passage, he describes and evaluates the state of those sages who have attained 'extinction' (*fanā'*):

They become intoxicated with such an intoxication that the ruling authority of their rational faculty is overthrown. Hence one of them says, "I am the Real!" (*anā'l-Haqq*), another, "Glory be to me, how great is my station!"[35] ... When this state gets the upper hand, it is called "extinction" in relation to the one who possesses it. Or rather, it is called "extinction from extinction", since the possessor of the state

---

33. Basis translates *upādhi*: 'Having in his person attained the deathless element which has no "basis", by making real the casting out of "basis", the Perfect Buddha, of no outflows, teaches the griefless, stainless state.' *Itivuttaka*, 62 (p. 82 of *Buddhist Texts Through the Ages*).

34. *Satasāhasrika*, LIII, f.279–283. Cited in *Buddhist Texts Through the Ages*, op. cit., pp. 174–175.

35. These are famous theopathic utterances (*shathiyāt*), by Mansūr al-Hallūj and Bāyazīd al-Bastāmī, respectively.

is extinct from himself and from his own extinction. For
he is conscious neither of himself in that state, nor of his
own unconsciousness of himself. If he were conscious of
his own unconsciousness, then he would [still] be conscious
of himself. In relation to the one immersed in it, this state
is called "unification" (*ittihād*) according to the language
of metaphor, or is called "declaring God's unity" (*tawhīd*)
according to the language of reality.[36]

The paradoxes uttered by the Buddha—as well as the identification
of the Buddha with the *Dharma*, or with Suchness, or *Nirvāna*,
etc.—might be seen as expressions of a *tawhīd* at once radical
and mystical, which is strictly predicated on extinction, *nirvāna*,
precisely: *ni* = 'out'; *vāna* = 'blowing', the idea being akin to a
flame being blown out by the wind. If Buddhist teachings are
read in the light of the chasm which separates language—and
with it, all formal concepts—from the reality consummated
through enlightenment, many puzzling paradoxes will be grasped
as inevitable shadows cast on the plane of thought by that which
deconstructs all thought, and negates the limitations of specific
consciousness: the negation of these limitations of specificity
implies the affirmation of liberating infinity. Whatever can be
distinctively perceived by the mind is other than the ultimate truth,
and is thus to be relinquished. Thought has to give way to being; in
other words, 'mental fabrication', to quote the *Avatamsaka Sutra*,
is to give way to a state of enlightened being:

> Having no doubt as to truth,
> Forever ending mental fabrication,
> Not producing a discriminating mind:
> This is awareness of enlightenment.[37]

The fact that this absence of 'discrimination' is far from a kind of
vacuity or thoughtlessness in the conventional sense is brought
home by the Sutra of Hui-neng.[38] Referring to the perfect wisdom

---

36. *The Niche of Lights*, op. cit., pp. 17–18.

37. *The Flower Ornament Scripture—A Translation of the Avatamsaka Sutra*,
op. cit., p. 292.

38. This sutra has the distinction of being 'the only sutra spoken by a native of
China', according to Wong Mou-lam, translator of this sutra. The name 'sutra' is
normally applied only to the sermons of the Buddha, and this shows the high esteem in which this discourse is held in Ch'an (Zen in Japan) Buddhism.

of *prajñā*, or the ultimate state of enlightenment, the word 'thought-lessness' is in fact used:

> To obtain liberation is to attain *samādhi* of *prajñā*, which is thoughtlessness. What is thoughtlessness? Thoughtlessness is to see and to know all *dharmas* with a mind free from attachment. When in use it pervades everywhere, and yet it sticks nowhere ... But to refrain from thinking of anything, so that all thoughts are suppressed, is to be *dharma*-ridden, and this is an erroneous view.[39]

* * *

As mentioned in the introduction, it would not be appropriate to compare Buddhist doctrine with Islamic dogma, as if they were situated on the same plane. It is *ma'rifa*, spiritual wisdom, within Islam, and not so much *'aqīda*, its formal creed, which can be fruitfully compared to Buddhist doctrine. But inasmuch as *ma'rifa*, as expounded by such authorities as al-Ghazālī, is in complete harmony with the Qur'ān and the Prophetic Sunna, the spiritual concordances which one can find between Islamic spirituality and Buddhism helps to uncover the transcendent common ground between Islam as such—and not simply its metaphysical dimensions—and Buddhism as such.

Baqā' of the 'Enlightened Ones'

Returning to the idea of the nonexistence of the 'enlightened ones', in the following citation from the immensely influential 'Diamond Sūtra' of the Mahayana tradition, we see that the enlightened ones do exist, but that their true reality is sustained not by themselves, but by the pure Absolute, referred to in our opening citation from the *Udāna* as the 'noncompound': *asamskrta*.

> This *dharma* which the *Tathāgata* has fully known or demonstrated—it cannot be grasped, it cannot be talked about, it is neither a *dharma* nor a no-*dharma*. And why? Because an Absolute exalts the holy persons (*asamskrtaprabhāvitā hy āryā-pudgalā*).[40]

Here, again, one can make use of the Sufi concept of *baqā'*, or subsistence: those who exist subsequent to the experience of extinction

---

39. *The Diamond Sutra and The Sutra of Hui-Neng*, op. cit., p. 85.
40. *Diamond Sutra*, cited in E. Conze, *Buddhist Texts*, op. cit,. p. 36

are sustained only by the reality of God, not by their own existence. This whole doctrine derives its Qur'ānic orthodoxy from, among others, the verse cited earlier: *Everything thereon is passing away* (fān); *and there subsists* (yabqā) *only the Face of your Lord, Owner of Majesty and Glory* (55:26–27). The mystic who has undergone extinction has, by that very fact, also concretely realized the nonexistence of all things other than God, all things that are in a state of 'passing away' even while apparently subsisting. Having died to his own illusory existence, it is God's 'Face', alone, that subsists; and it is through that subsistence that the individual himself subsists—his 'face' or essence being in reality not 'his' but God's: nothing exists, as we saw earlier, apart from God and the Face/Essence of God, which shines through all things.

In this light, it is possible to see why it is that, on the one hand, the Buddha states that he has 'known' the *Dharma*, and on the other, that it cannot be grasped, talked about, and that in fact it is 'neither a *dharma* nor a no-*dharma*': insofar as all such characterizations of the Absolute derive from the individual stand-point, and insofar as the individual's existence is strictly illusory on its own account, all such characterizations of the Absolute cannot but assume the nature of an illusion, or at best a 'provisional means' (*upāya*) of expressing the inexpressible. In the Diamond Sutra we read the paradox that the truth declared by the Buddha is neither real nor unreal:

> Subhuti, the *Tathāgata* is he who declares that which is true, he who declares that which is fundamental, he who declares that which is ultimate ... Subhuti, that truth to which the *Tathāgata* has attained is neither real nor unreal.[41]

The 'truth' which can be defined in terms of a polarity constituted by reality versus unreality cannot be the ultimate truth. That alone is truth which transcends the domain in which such dualistic notions can be posited. It is not a truth which can be qualified as real, for its very truth must be absolutely one with reality: its own 'suchness' must be its entire truth and reality, and cannot be known as 'real' or 'true' in any final sense except by itself.

The following dialogue between the same disciple, Subhuti, and the Buddha brings home the paradox of this Absolute that can only be known by itself, by its own 'Suchness' (*tathatā*):

---

41. *The Diamond Sutra and the Sutra of Hui-Neng*, op. cit., p. 32.

52

> Subhuti: 'If, O Lord, outside Suchness no separate *dharma* can be apprehended, then what is that *dharma* that will stand firmly in suchness, or that will know this full enlightenment, or that will demonstrate this *dharma*?'
>
> Buddha: 'Outside Suchness no separate *dharma* can be apprehended, that could stand firmly in Suchness. The very Suchness, to begin with, cannot be apprehended, how much less that which can stand firmly in it. Suchness does not know full enlightenment, and on the dharmic plane no one can be found who has either known full enlightenment, will know it, or does know it. Suchness does not demonstrate *dharma*, and on the dharmic plane, no one can be found who could demonstrate it.'[42]

Nobody, not even the Buddha, can 'demonstrate' the Absolute, because such a demonstration requires concepts and language, and the Absolute/Suchness transcends all such concepts. For this reason, the Buddha stresses the need to be stripped of all 'thought-coverings' (*acitta-āvaranah*): thought, by its very nature, 'covers' and thus obscures the source or substance or root of its own consciousness. It is only when thought assumes the nature of a transparent veil over its own substratum of consciousness that authentic wisdom is attained. If thought is 'seen through', then the thinker, the agent of thought, is in a sense extinguished before the source and goal of thought. To say 'thinker' is to deny the sole reality of the absolute nature of consciousness—whence the paradox that the *Dharma* is both 'known' by the Buddha and unknown by him; it is both attained and not attained:

> Therefore, O Sariputra, it is because of his nonattainment-ness [sic] that a Bodhisattva, through having relied on the perfection of wisdom, dwells without thought-coverings … and in the end he attains to *Nirvana*.[43]

Let us again turn to al-Ghazālī, who provides a corresponding formulation, referring not to 'thought-coverings' but to 'individual faculties'. The highest spiritual sciences (*al-maʿārif*, pl. of *maʿrifa*) are only revealed to the individual through spiritual states of 'unveiling' (*mukāshafa*), and these, in turn, are predicated upon the extinction

---

42. *Prajñāpāramitā Sutra*, A/27:453, cited in ibid., p. 37.
43. *Heart Sutra*, verses 37–43, cited in ibid., p. 93.

of the individual's consciousness. *Fanā'* is the essential pre-requisite of this unveiling because:

> The contingencies of the ego, together with its passions, exert an attraction towards the sensible world, which is a world of error and illusion. The Real unveils itself completely at death, with the cessation of the power of the senses and the imagination which turn the heart towards this lower world ... *Fanā'* refers to a state wherein the senses are pacified, not preoccupied; and the imagination is in repose, not generating confusion.[44]

This may be seen as a mystical commentary on the following verses of the Qur'ān:

> *Whoso migrates for the sake of God will find much refuge and abundance in the earth, and whoso forsakes his home, being a fugitive to God and His Messenger, and death overtakes him, his reward is then incumbent upon God. God is ever Forgiving, Merciful* (4:100).

The death of the body is prefigured in that death of the lower soul in the state of *fanā'*.

Let us return to Nāgārjuna's fundamental distinction between the 'two truths', as this will help place in context the concordance between the two traditions as regards the conception of the pure Absolute: 'The teaching of the doctrine by the Buddhas is based upon two truths: truth relating to worldly convention and truth in terms of ultimate fruit.'[45] It is on the level of conventional truth (*samvrti-satyam*), that one can situate the explanations pertaining to the whole process of dependent origination, impermanence, and suffering. The truth or reality pertaining to 'ultimate fruit' (*paramārtha*), however, transcends this entire domain. The word 'fruit' (*artha*, Pali: *attha*), which can also be translated as consequence or result, draws our attention to the existential unfolding of reality consequent upon enlightenment: the discovery of 'the truth' or 'reality' (*satyam*)[46] is not to be found on the level of

---

44. See his treatise *Kitāb al-Arba'īn fī usūl al-dīn* (Beirut: Dar al-Afaq al-Abadiyya, 1979), pp. 44–45; and for discussion on this and other similar passages from al-Ghazālī's works, see Farid Jabre, *La Notion de la Ma'rifa chez Ghazālī* (Paris: Traditions les Lettres Orientales, 1958), p. 125.

45. From his *Mūlamadhyamakakārikā*, 24:8, cited by David Kalupahana, *Nāgārjuna—The Philosophy of the Middle Way*, op. cit., p. 331.

46. As in the Arabic word *haqq*, the Sanskrit *satyam* can be translated both in terms of reality and truth.

formal thought and by the empirically defined individual; rather, it is the indescribable 'fruit' of the experience of enlightenment. The positive content of this enlightenment—absolute Reality—is thus not denied when the formal designations of that Reality are undermined, contradicted or ignored. What is contradicted by the Buddha is the idea that the ultimate Reality can be adequately designated, contained, and still less realized, on the level of formal thought by the individual, both being bound up by relativity of *nama-rupa* (name and form). This explains why in some texts even the idea of ultimate reality being uncompounded is contradicted:

> The Buddhas' reality is subtle and hard to fathom;
> No words or speech can reach it.
> It is not compounded or uncompounded;
> Its essential nature is void and formless.[47]

Referring to the ultimate reality as uncompounded is an error, not because the ultimate reality is in fact compounded, but because the very fact of verbally designating it as uncompounded is already tantamount to an act of compounding. There is the uncompounded reality, on the one hand, and the description of it as uncompounded: putting the two together means that one has left the presence of the uncompounded and embraced the compounded. The final verse in the passage quoted, 'Its essential nature is void and formless', could just as well be contradicted, for the very same reason as one contradicts the idea of reality being uncompounded. Holding on to the idea of reality being void or formless itself undermines the voidness of that reality, and acts as a mental barrier preventing one from being submerged in it. Again, according to *The Flower Ornament Scripture*:

> Things expressed by words
> Those of lesser wisdom wrongly discriminate
> And therefore create barriers
> And don't comprehend their own minds.
> ...
> If one can see the Buddha,
> One's mind will have no grasping;
> Such a person can then perceive
> Truth as the Buddha knows it.[48]

---

47. *The Flower Ornament Scripture*, op. cit., p. 290.
48. Ibid., p. 376.

In terms of Islamic spirituality, the very thought of *tawhīd* on the mental plane can itself become an obstacle in the path of spiritual realization of *tawhīd*, a realization which is predicated not just on the elimination of all mental constructs, but also on the extinction of individual consciousness. Any concept—even true ones—will entrench that consciousness, and thus is 'wrong' from the higher point of view of the reality which transcends all concepts. Buddhist conceptions of the Absolute are thus fashioned according to this paradoxical requirement: to conceive of the Absolute in a way which reveals the ultimate inadequacy of all concepts, and which focuses all spiritual aspiration on making a leap from the plane of finite thought to the plane of infinite reality. Another way of putting this is to say: 'Those who seek the truth shouldn't seek anything'.[49] Seeking a 'thing' will ensure that the truth of all things will not be found. Even having a view of a 'thing', will prevent one from 'seeing' all things:

No view is seeing
Which can see all things;
If one has any views about things,
This is not seeing anything.[50]

This attitude may be summed up succinctly in the words which come a few verses later: 'divorcing the concept of things'.[51] It is not the ultimate nature of things that is negated, rather, what is negated is their susceptibility to adequate conceptualization: that ultimate nature can be delivered or glimpsed only in a flash of pure, supra-conceptual, awareness. So the best teaching, the best 'concept', is that which predisposes one to this mode of intuitive cognition, which arises more out of a state of inner being than of formal thought. The ultimate Reality, far from being negated in this perspective, is affirmed in the deepest way in which it can be affirmed: by negating all that can in any way claim to be the Real on the level of thought and language, 'name and form' (*nama-rupa*): in Islamic terms: *lā ilāha illa'Llāh*. To apply the distinction of Nāgārjuna between 'conventional truth' (*samvrti-satyam*) and 'ultimate fruit' (*paramārtha*), one might say that 'divorcing the concept of things' is a process which must lead from the domain of relative truth, where the concept of things is a veil, to the domain

---

49. This is from the *Vimalakirti Scripture*, as cited by Cleary in ibid., p. 35.
50. Ibid., p. 376.
51. Ibid., p. 377.

56

of ultimate truth, wherein resides the transcendent reality of That which is only ever partially conceptualised in the lower domain. The 'divorce' in question, then, is not to be applied to ultimate Reality, but to all things which would attempt to imprison its infinitude within the finite framework of thought.

The Diamond Sutra contains the pith of this teaching, expressing the imperative of the divorce in question in simple but powerful imagery. These images are aimed at inducing a state of mind and being which is referred to simply in terms of two imperatives: 'detachment from appearances—abiding in real truth.' To be detached from what *appears* is practically tantamount to realization of what never *disappears*, that which eternally transcends the realm of appearances, 'the real truth'.

> Thus shall ye think of all this fleeting world:
> A star at dawn, a bubble in the stream;
> A flash of lightning in a summer cloud,
> A flickering lamp, a phantom and a dream.[52]

This might be compared to such verses of the Qur'ān as the following:

> *Know that the life of the world is only play, and idle talk, and pomp, and boasting between you, and rivalry in wealth and children; as the likeness of vegetation after rain, whose growth is pleasing to the farmer, but afterwards it dries up and you see it turning yellow, then it becomes straw...* (57:20).

However many long years are passed in the 'life of this world', they will appear as less than a single day when the end of this life is reached:

> *They ask you of the Hour: when will it come to pass? Why— what can you say about it? Unto your Lord belongs [knowledge of] the term thereof. You are but a warner unto him who fears it. On the day when they behold it, it will be as if they had but tarried for an evening or the morn thereof* (79:43–46).

The Prophetic saying 'All men are asleep; when they die, they wake up', can be read as a profound commentary on these verses.[53]

---

52. *The Diamond Sutra*, op. cit., p. 53.

53. Though not found in the canonical sources, this saying is often quoted by the spiritual authorities of Islam. Al-Ghazālī, for example, cites it several times in his

We hope that these observations have helped to demonstrate that at the metaphysical level the two traditions are indeed oriented to the One and only Reality, however much the strictly 'theological' conception of this Reality in Islam differs from the mystical conceptions within Buddhism. We now need to address the question of whether this ultimate Reality is also the object of worship in Buddhism, failing which the Muslim scholar may conclude that, even if the Buddhists appear to have a metaphysical or philosophical appreciation of the oneness of ultimate Reality, they nevertheless do not worship this Absolute, and thus cannot be included in the sphere of 'true believers'.

Worship of the One

In Islam *shirk* is not only the doctrinal error of 'associating partners' with God, or ascribing divinity to idols; it is also the wilful 'sin' of worshipping something other than God: *And whoever has hope in the meeting of his Lord, let him act virtuously, and make none sharer of the worship due to his Lord* (18:110).

When, therefore, the Muslim reads the Buddhist testimony of the 'Triple Refuge', he is likely to regard it as an act of *shirk*: 'I take refuge in the Buddha, the *Dharma* and the *Sangha*'. The Buddha is but a man; the *Dharma*, but the teaching, the law, or the norm; and the *Sangha*, but a community of monks: where is mention of the ultimate Reality in which one must take refuge, to which devotion and worship is due? To answer this question, we would do well to return to the citation above, where *Dharma* was translated as Reality. The word comprises several meanings, including: teaching, norm, law, truth, reality. The difficulty of defining it precisely is revealed by the Buddha himself:

> This Reality [*Dhamma*, Pali for *Dharma*] that I have reached is profound, hard to see, hard to understand, excellent, pre-eminent, beyond the sphere of thinking, subtle, and to be penetrated by the wise alone.[54]

Ihyā'. Mohammed Rustom in his article notes the following instances in the Beirut, 1997 edition of the *Ihyā'*: 1:15; 3:381; 4:246, 260. See M. Rustom, 'Psychology, eschatology, and imagination in Mulla Sadra Shirazi's commentary on the *hadith* of awakening', in *Islam and Science*, vol. 5, no.1, 1997, p. 10.

54. Cited from the *Majjhima Nikāya*, in *Some Sayings of the Buddha According to the Pali Canon*, tr. F.L. Woodward (London: Oxford University Press, 1925), p. 4.

The most immediate meaning of the word *Dharma* relates more to the teaching, the doctrine, and the law or norm stemming therefrom; but it can also refer to the ultimate content of the doctrine, that in which both the doctrine and the law culminate, and of which the Buddha himself is but the conveyor. This higher metaphysical meaning of *Dharma* emerges if we look at the Mahayana scriptures, and particularly at the conception of the three 'bodies' of the Buddha. This will help us to see the extent to which *Dharma* in its higher meaning of truth/reality, can be grasped as the same ultimate Truth/Reality to which Muslims refer as *al-Haqīqa* or *al-Haqq*. It can also help us to see that the Buddha in whom one takes 'refuge' is by no means to be identified exhaustively with the sage Shakyamuni, who was but the messenger, bearer of the message of the *Dharma* before which he himself is effaced. This subordination of the Buddha to the *Dharma* is explicitly taught in the following Mahayana Sūtra:

> Those who by my form did see me, and those who followed me by my voice, wrong are the efforts they engaged in; me those people will not see. From the *Dharma* one should see the Buddha, for the *dharma*-bodies are the guides.[55]

Two points should be stressed here: the deluded state of those who attach excessive significance to the human form of the Buddha; and the emphasis on seeing the Buddha in the light of the *Dharma*, rather than vice versa. The ontological precedence of the *Dharma* is thus affirmed here. Then, in relation to the description of the '*dharma*-bodies' as 'guides', these bodies of the *Dharma* manifest at different levels in the form of so many types of Buddha: the human level (*nirmāna-kāya*, or 'transformation-body'); the celestial level (*sambhoga-kāya* or 'felicity-body'); and the divine or Absolute level (*dharma-kāya*, translated as 'Being-body'). One can speak relatively easily of the first two 'bodies' of the Buddha in terms of earthly manifestation and celestial archetype. In Islam, the distinction would correspond to the Prophet as the particular man Muhammad b. 'Abd Allah, on the one hand, and the pre-human archetypal reality of the Prophetic substance, alluded to in these famous words of the Prophet: 'I was a Prophet when Adam was [still] between water and clay'.[56]

---

55. *Vajracchedikā*, 26a, b. Cited in *Buddhist Texts Through the Ages*, op. cit., p. 144.

56. The most strongly authenticated version of this saying is as follows: The Prophet was asked when he became a Prophet. He replied: 'When Adam was between spirit

Buddha in the Light of *Dharma*

However, it is rather more difficult to make sense of the *dharma-kāya*: how can the ultimate reality be 'embodied' in the form of a Buddha? We could argue, applying strict Buddhist logic: it is not, and cannot be. For such an embodiment would perforce violate the utterly non-compound reality of the Void. The same paradox is observed in one of the names of the Buddha, *Shūnyamurtī*: manifestation of the Void. The Buddha manifests an image or reflection or intimation of that which cannot ever be subject to manifestation except on pain of ceasing to be the Void, for the void is devoid of manifestation, by definition. This *dharma-kāya* can thus be understood as a degree of reality which can be conceived only as the Absolute, but not in any sense as a manifestation thereof: we propose that the word '*kāya*', body or vehicle is thus to be taken metaphorically and not literally. *Dharma* in this ultimate sense cannot be equated with any specific manifestation, however exalted; rather, it is the Principle of manifestation, and must therefore remain supra-manifest. What is manifested cannot be the Absolute as such, but rather, that aspect of the Absolute which is susceptible of manifestation. If the manifestation of the celestial Buddha (*sambhoga-kāya*), and a fortiori, the human Buddha (*nirmana-kāya*) be mistaken for the Absolute then, instead of revealing the path to the Absolute, these relative forms become veils obscuring It. We would argue also that the very fact that the death of the Buddha is referred to as his *parinirvana*, the ultimate or greatest Nirvana, demonstrates in its own way that the Absolute can only be realized in the ultimate sense subsequent to the termination of the manifestation of the human form of the Buddha.

According to Hui-neng (d. 713):[57] 'For whatever can be named leads to dualism, and Buddhism is not dualistic. To take hold of this non-duality of truth is the aim of Zen'.[58] In similar vein, the teacher of Hui-neng, Hung-jen, writes: 'One will not get rid of birth and death if one constantly thinks of other Bud-

---

and body'. See Tirmidhī, *Manāqib*, 1; and Ibn Hanbal, 1, 281, *et passim*.

57. The 6th patriarch of the Ch'an/Zen school, who was, according to Suzuki, 'the real Chinese founder of Zen'. D.T. Suzuki, *Essays in Zen*, op. cit., vol. 1, p. 108

58. Ibid., vol. 1, p. 212.

dhas. However, if one retains one's mindfulness,[59] one is sure to reach the Further Shore.' He then quotes the Buddha's words from the *Vajraccedika-prajnāpāramitā Sūtra*: 'If any one wishes to see me in form, or to seek me in sound, this person is treading an evil path and he cannot see the *Tathāgata*.'[60] The reality of the *Tathāgata*, 'the one thus gone', is the Buddha-nature, to which each being has access, but only insofar as one is liberated from all attachment to form, even, ironically, the form of the Buddha himself. One understands from this why the Zen masters transmitted the saying: 'If you see the Buddha on the road, kill him!' In the words of the *Flower Ornament Scripture*:

> Since sentient beings are thus,
> So also are the Buddhas:
> Buddhas and Buddha-teachings
> Intrinsically have no existence.[61]

And again:

> Even if one always looked at the Buddha
> For a hundred thousand eons,
> Not according to the absolute truth
> But looking at the savior of the world,
> Such a person is grasping appearances
> And increasing the web of ignorance and delusion,
> Bound in the prison of birth and death,
> Blind, unable to see the Buddha.
> …

---

59. Mindfulness is a perfect translation of the Arabic *taqwā*. The latter term, though, strongly implies that the object of mindfulness is God. Given, however, that in Buddhism one's mindfulness is a form of permanent recollectedness of the Dharma in the very midst of all outward activities, the two terms can be seen to be indicating the same state of mind: an awareness of the Absolute which is not interrupted by one's engagement with the relative. The Qur'ān refers to *rijāl*, true men, *who are not distracted from the remembrance of God either by trade nor commerce* (24:36). See below for discussion of the remembrance of God.

60. From the translation of Hung-Jen's discourse on meditation by W. Pachow, in his *Chinese Buddhism—Aspects of Interaction and Reinterpretation* (Lanham: University Press of America, 1980), p. 40.

61. *The Flower Ornament Scripture*, op. cit., p. 450.

Ordinary people seeing things
Just pursue the forms
And don't realize things are formless:
Because of this they don't see Buddha.[62]

Thus, it cannot be said that the Buddha is 'worshipped' either in the two forms of his human or celestial 'bodies' or in the form of 'his' divine body, the *dharma-kāya*. If the latter truly pertains to the *Dharma* as such, then it cannot be appropriated by any being; and if it is so appropriated, then it cannot be the *Dharma*. As we shall argue below, in connection with the 'remembrance of God', the object of devotion may well be the image of the Buddha, or a *Bodhisattva*, in the first instance, but in good Buddhist logic, this object is rendered transparent, given its 'emptiness of self', thus allowing free passage to the only reality which is fully itself, possessed of absolute 'suchness', the *Dharma*.

The following synonyms for the *Dharma*, given by D.T. Suzuki in his comparison of terms used to designate God or ultimate Reality in different religious traditions, might be of use in our reflections: *Prajna* ('pure consciousness'), *Tathatā* ('suchness'), *Bodhi* ('enlightenment'), *Buddha* ('enlightened one').[63] Similarly, in relation to *Dharma-kāya*, Ananda Coomaraswamy gives these synonyms: *Ādi-Buddha* ('primordial' or 'Absolute' Buddha), also identified with *Vairocana*; *Svabhāvakāya* ('own-nature body'); *Tattva* ('essentiality'); *Shūnya* ('the Void'); *Nirvāna* ('extinctive bliss'); *Samādhikāya* ('rapture-body'); *Bodhi* ('wisdom'); *Prajnā* ('pure consciousness').[64]

The *Dharma* in question at this transcendent level, then, is not simply bound up with subjective mystical experience; it is also one with the ultimate objective nature of consciousness and being—it refers both to an objective transcendent principle as well as to a subjective state accessible by dint of the immanence of that principle within all that exists. Although this identification of the Absolute in terms of the *Dharma-kāya* is stressed within Mahayana Buddhism, and particularly in the Yogacara school which developed the doctrine of the three 'bodies' of the Buddha subsequent to the 4th cen-

---

62. Ibid., p. 373.

63. D.T. Suzuki, 'The Buddhist Conception of Reality', in Frederick Franck, ed., *The Buddhist Eye* (Bloomington: World Wisdom, 2004), p. 85.

64. Ananda Coomaraswamy, *Buddha and the Gospel of Buddhism* (New Jersey: Citadel Press, 1988) p. 239.

tury CE, it has been argued by Edward Conze that 'there is nothing really new about it … The identification of one side of the Buddha with the Dharma had often been made in the first period [of Buddhism] and is of the essence of Buddhism.'[65]

To speak about 'one side of the Buddha' needs to be nuanced somewhat, for what is really meant is surely one aspect of the consciousness of the 'Awakened one': the Buddha insofar he is identified with the content of his enlightenment. Then, the *Dharma* as Transcendent Being and source of life and consciousness will be grasped as That of which the Buddha's enlightenment is an aspect: 'From the *Dharma* one should see the Buddha' and not vice versa, as we saw above.

Marco Pallis, in his important essay, 'Dharma and Dharmas as Principle of Inter-religious Communication', would thus appear to be justified in stressing this concept as a bridge linking diverse religious traditions. The key sentence, as regards the metaphysical point we have been trying to make here, is the following: 'If Dharma corresponds, on the one hand, to the absoluteness and infinitude of Essence, the dharmas for their part correspond to the relativity and contingency of the accidents.'[66]

The *Dharma* can thus be understood in two distinct senses, one philosophical or ontological, and the other pedagogical or practical. In the first sense, it refers to what Islamic thought understands as the Essence (*al-Dhāt*): the Essence of God is the Absolute (in theological terms) and the sole Reality (in spiritual terms). All particular essences are relative (in theological terms) or illusory (in spiritual terms). In the pedagogical or practical sense, the *Dharma* as teaching, law, norm, etc., can be seen to correspond to the *Sharī'a* (exoterically) and the *Tarīqa* (esoterically). Taken together in both senses, ontological and practical, then, the single term *Dharma* in Buddhism might be seen to correspond approximately to the ternary in Islam: *al-Haqīqa, al-Tarīqa, al-Sharī'a*: Essential Reality, Spiritual Path, Religious Law. All three of these terms are, in a certain sense summed up in the divine Name, *al-Haqq*, 'the True', or 'the Real', which might be seen as perhaps the divine Name most closely corresponding to *Dharma*, inasmuch as the notion of obligation and right, hence duty and law, so central to the meaning of *dharma*, are

---

65. E. Conze, *Buddhism—A Short History* (Oxford: Oneworld, 2000), p. 51.

66. M. Pallis, *A Buddhist Spectrum* (London: George Allen & Unwin, 1980), p. 103.

also implied in *al-Haqq*, one of whose principal connotations is indeed that of a 'right' which is 'due' as an obligation. Both *al-Haqq* and the *Dharma*, then, imply at one and the same time the highest truth and reality in metaphysical terms, and also the deepest commitment to that truth, in human terms.

Remembrance of God

As regards worship, again it is a question of seeing that the two traditions come together at key points in respect of essence, and are widely divergent as regards form. This essence is cultivation of the consciousness of the Absolute, expressed in Islam as *dhikr Allāh*, remembrance/invocation/consciousness of God. The *dhikr* of God is described as the very *raison d'être* of all forms of prayer; this is made clear in the Qur'ānic verse in which God says: '*Establish the prayer for the sake of My remembrance*' (20:14). The very purpose and goal of the prayer, its spiritual value and substance, is thus the remembrance of God. If formal or canonical prayer constitutes the core of religious practice, the *dhikru'Llāh* is, as the Qur'ān puts it very simply, *akbar*, that is, 'greater' or 'greatest': '*Truly, prayer keeps [one] away from lewdness and iniquity, but the remembrance of God is greater*' (29:45).

The Arabic word *dhikr* comprises two essential meanings, that of remembrance and that of invocation; it refers, therefore, to both the goal and the means: both the principle of permanent consciousness of the Absolute, and the means of realising that consciousness. This means of realisation is centred on the methodic invocation of the Name (or Names) of God, and most especially, the supreme Name of God in Islam, *Allāh*. Similarly, in Buddhism—and in particular in the later Mahayana schools—the invocation of the Name (or Names) of the Absolute figures as the means of salvation *par excellence*. Buddhism developed a panoply of disciplines and techniques of prayer, meditation, and incantation, inheriting also from Hinduism the practice of *japa-yoga*, the way of repetition/invocation, which it articulated in numerous ways. While it would be unjustified to reduce all of these techniques of prayer and meditation to invocation alone, it is nonetheless important to underline the extraordinary parallels between the Islamic tradition of *dhikr* and those schools of thought within Buddhism which likewise regard the practice of invocatory prayer to be the quintessence of all possible prayer. It suffices for our purposes to cite a few sayings from the Japanese authority, Honen (d. 1212), founder of the Jodo-shu, 'Pure Land', school of Mahayana Buddhism which is arguably one of the closest of all Buddhist schools to the Islamic contemplative tradition as regards invocatory prayer. It should also be noted that the Vajrayāna school, referred to in the introduction, is often referred to in the Tibetan tradition as the Mantrayāna ('vehicle of the mantra') given the centrality of invocatory formulae in this branch of Buddhism.

In the Pure Land school, the Buddha of Infinite Light, *Amitābha* (*Omitofu* in Chinese, *Amida* in Japanese), assumes the role of saviour, and is invoked as such. One is 'saved' by *Amida* by being resurrected after death in his 'Pure land', the *Sukhāvatī* or 'Paradise of Bliss', descriptions of which closely resemble those of the Qur'ānic Paradise. This salvific grace is the result of the vows taken by *Dharmakāra*, according to the Sutra of 'Eternal Life', the Chinese translation of which formed the chief basis of the Shin school within Pure Land Buddhism, both in China and in Japan (where it became known as *Jodo Shin*).[67] In light of our earlier discussion about the 'bodies' of the Buddha, it should be clear that what is being invoked is not the human form of the Buddha, but '*Amitābha*' as such, that is: infinite Light,[68] streaming forth from the Absolute, a Light which both enlightens and saves. It is thus as if the two divine Names, *al-Nūr* ('The Light') and *al-Rahīm* ('The Merciful') were synthesised[69] and invoked as a single Name. According to the mythological[70] account of the saving 'vow' of *Amida*, *Shakyamuni* speaks of having attained Buddhahood in the infinitely distant past—ten 'kalpas' ago, each kalpa being 432 million years.[71] Here, the number of years is clearly symbolic: we are being invited to enter into a timeless domain, a distant past or origin—a

67. D. T. Suzuki, *On Indian Mahayana Buddhism* (New York: Harper & Row, 1968), p. 137.

68. The word *Amitābha* is also interpreted to include the aspect of 'infinite life', *Amitāyus*. Both Light and Life are infinite, and this degree of the Buddha-Reality is clearly transcendent and cannot be identified with any relative manifestations thereof within samsara or, in Islamic terms, the 'created' world.

69. Or three, including *al-Hayy*, the eternally Living, if we include the '*Amitāyus*' dimension of *Amitābha*.

70. Taking this word in its positive sense: a myth is a story expressing a mystery—both words are derived from the same Greek root, 'mu', meaning 'mute' or 'silent'. In the face of a divine mystery, the most appropriate response is to remain 'silent', but the 'myth' gives provisional and approximate expression to the mystery which is ultimately inexpressible.

71. Kenryo Kanamatsu, *Naturalness—A Classic of Shin Buddhism* (Bloomington: World Wisdom, 2002), p. 17.

'pre-eternity', referred to in Islam as *Azal*. Pre-eternity is at one with post-eternity (*Abad*), or simply, eternity as such; and thus what is being alluded to in these references to the unimaginable 'past' is in fact an eternal principle, above and beyond time.

This 'primordial' or 'original' Buddha is also referred to as the *Ādi-Buddha*, which is also the 'Absolute' Buddha principle, since, as seen above, it is a synonym for the *Dharma-kāya* itself. If the *Ādi-Buddha* is the origin of all things, at the very beginning, it can correspond to what Muslims refer to in terms of the divine Name, *al-Awwal*, ('The First'); and, metaphysically, 'The First' must also be 'The Last' (*al-Ākhir*): alpha and omega are in principle identical, and can be distinguished as origin and consummation only from the point of view of time itself; in themselves, they are not other than outward expressions of the principle of eternity transcending time altogether. This is succinctly expressed by a contemporary Jodo scholar, commenting upon the words of *Shakymuni* in which he describes his primordial 'enlightenment': 'This is the Eternal *I am* that speaks through the *I am* that is in me'.[72] The Buddha is thus 'speaking' not as an individual or on his own behalf, but as the mouthpiece or transmitter of a universal reality. 'His' enlightenment aeons ago is a mythical way of referring to enlightenment as such, or the source of all enlightenment, Light as such, which is eternal, thus absolute and infinite, for, as Kanamatsu says: 'Amida, the Infinite Being, is perfect and eternal.'[73]

Likewise, in respect of the 'vow' taken by Amida not to enter enlightenment until all beings are saved, this can be understood in terms of universal principles, abstracted from their mythological garb: 'Amida is ... Heart of our hearts. He is the All-Feeling Compassionate Heart ... Amida is the Eternal Saving Will, the eternally working Original Vow.'[74] This compassionate 'vow'—normally expressed as a vow not to enter final enlightenment until all beings are saved—can be seen as analogous to the metaphor used by God in the Qur'ān to describe His mercy: *Your Lord has written Mercy upon His own Self* (6:12). Also to be noted in this connection is

---

72. Ibid., p. 12. One is reminded here of what in Islam is called a *hadīth qudsī*, a 'holy saying', the speaker of which is God Himself, but delivered through the Prophet as a medium. These sayings are distinct from the Qur'ān, but their agent is still God Himself, and by no means the Prophet.

73. Ibid., p. 13.

74. Ibid., p. 85.

the verse: *Call upon Allāh or call upon al-Rahmān* (the 'All-Compassionate') (17:110). One sees here that the intrinsic nature of the Absolute is saving compassion; the invocation of the 'name' of the Absolute is thus absolutely salvific. We shall return to the theme of mercy and compassion shortly. But for now, we should note that the Prophet of Islam expressed a sentiment analogous to the vow of Amida, alluding to his prerogative to intercede for sinners. In relation to the verse of the Qur'ān which says: *And your Lord shall give you, and you will be content* (93:5), he said: 'I shall not be content for as long as a single member of my community (*umma*) is in the Fire.'[75] Given that the Prophet was sent as a *'mercy to the whole of creation'* (21:107) his 'community' can be interpreted to mean all peoples—and even all 'beings', as in the vow of Amida—and not just 'Muslims' in the narrow sense of the word.

Tariki and *Tawakkul*

In the Amidist tradition these principles are operatively expressed in the *Nembutsu*, the invocation of the formula: *namu Amida Butsu*, 'veneration to Amitābha Buddha'. Honen calls upon his followers to 'cease not the practice of the Nembutsu even for a moment';[76] 'seeing that the practice may be carried on, whether walking, standing, sitting or lying, whensoever and wheresoever one may be ... the Nembutsu is called an easy practice'.[77] One is reminded here of the verse of the Qur'ān: *Truly in the creation of the heavens and the earth, and in the alternation between night and day, there are signs for possessors of substance, those who invoke God standing, sitting and reclining on their sides* ... (3:190–191).

Honen tells his followers that there is no more effective discipline than that of the *Nembutsu* if one wishes to attain enlightenment and to be reborn in the 'Land of Perfect Bliss'. 'All the other disciplines', he says, 'are effective for their respective purposes, but not for birth in the Pure Land.'[78] Likewise, we have such sayings as the following, from the Prophet, which refer to the practice of the *dhikr* as being the most efficacious of all forms of prayer and action:

---

75. Many sayings of a similar import are found in various collections. This particular saying is found in the collection of al-Daylamī.

76. *Honen, The Buddhist Saint: His Life and Teaching*, Shunjo, tr. H.H. Coates, R. Ishizuka (New York: Garland, 1981), vol. 2, p. 441.

77. Ibid., vol. 2, p. 460.

78. Ibid., vol. 2, p. 463.

'Shall I not tell you about the best and purest of your works for your Lord, and the most exalted of them in your ranks, and the work that is better for you than giving silver and gold, and better for you than encountering your enemy, with you striking their necks and them striking your necks?' The people addressed by him said: 'What is that, O messenger of God?' He said, 'The perpetual invocation of God'.[79]

The practice of the *Nembutsu* is strongly predicated upon the power of the 'absolutely Other', *tariki*, as opposed to one's own power, *jiriki*. One might argue that *tariki* is precisely what *tawakkul*, reliance or trust, means in Islam: one relies totally upon the grace and power of the 'Other', which is absolutely other than oneself. In this total trust, this gift of self to the Other, one sees the Islamic conception of *tawakkul* (and the meaning of 'Islam' itself, literally 'submission') also evoking the idea of *anattā*, no-self, in Buddhism: the totality of one's trust in, and submission to the Other disposes the self to a radical mode of self-effacement: one relies not on oneself but on the absolutely Other. In the Pure Land school, this faith in the Other is faith in the power of the grace emanating from Amida, principle of infinite light.

Both *tariki* and *tawakkul* are aimed at realizing in practical mode, the existential concomitant of the *anattā* doctrine: removal of self-centred consciousness, reliance on the Absolute, which is the absolutely 'Other'. Indeed, one can go further, and assert that *tawakkul* is not only governed by the same spiritual goal as that to which the *anattā* doctrine is attuned; the principle of *tawakkul* also makes explicit that which is logically necessary, while remaining unarticulated, in the earliest expressions of the *anattā* doctrine. For, as will be further argued below, it is logically impossible to overcome the sense of self by means of the self—there must be something radically 'other', utterly beyond the self, which, alone, enables one to transcend one's congenital sense of self-preoccupation. This self-preoccupation in turn generates a false sense of self-sufficiency. The authentic quality of self-sufficiency is the exclusive preserve of the one Reality; in the measure that the human soul attributes to itself this quality, it 'rebels' against the true nature of its own utter dependence on God as the Other, and rebels against the One which

---

79. Cited in *Al-Ghazālī: Invocations and Supplications* (Book IX of *Ihyā' 'ulūm al-dīn*), trans. K. Nakamura (Cambridge: Islamic Texts Society, 1990), p. 8. We have slightly modified the translation of the last sentence of the *hadīth*.

is, alone, truly 'Independent'; as is said in the Qur'ān: *Truly man is rebellious, in that he deems himself self-sufficient* (96:6–7).

The following passage from Kanamatsu's *Naturalness* will not only evoke the spiritual commentaries made upon the famous 'verse of light' (*āyat al-nūr*, 24:35) in the Qur'ān; it also shows the extent to which this tradition of Buddhism resonates with Islam's insistence upon the values of trust, faith, and unconditional submission to God:

> The lamp contains its oil, which it holds securely in its close grasp and guards from the least loss. Thus is it separate from all other objects around it and miserly. But when lit, it finds its meaning at once; its relation with all things far and near is established, and it freely sacrifices its fund of oil to feed the flame. Such a lamp is our self ... the lamp must give up its oil to the light and thus set free the implicit purpose it has ... This is emancipation ... The naturalness (*jen*) which Shinran[80] preached is nothing less than this emancipation of the self; a holy freedom through the melting of our self-power (*jiriki*) in the Other Power (*tariki*), through the surrender of our self-will (*hakarai*) to the Eternal Will ... This is what Shinran meant by declaring that the direct road to deliverance is absolute faith in Amida.[81]

Key to Salvation

The remembrance/invocation of God is referred to by Ibn 'Atā'Allāh al-Iskandarī (d. 1309), a major authority within Sufism, as 'The Key to Salvation': 'Verily, the remembrance of God Most High is the key to salvation and the lamp of souls ... the foundation of the Path and the pivotal support of realized sages ... liberation from ignorance and forgetfulness through the permanent presence of the heart with the Truth.'[82] Likewise, within Buddhism, the remembrance/invocation can be seen as, at least, a 'key to salvation', as was affirmed by the Dalai Lama. He was asked whether the invocation, *Om mani padme hum* (*Om*, jewel in the lotus, *hum*) would suffice by itself to take a man all the way to Deliverance. 'His Holiness replied that

---

80. Shinran (d. 1262) was the successor to Honen.

81. Kenryo Kanamatsu, *Naturalness*, op. cit., pp. 42–43.

82. Ibn 'Atā'Allāh al-Iskandarī, *The Key to Salvation—A Sufi Manual of Invocation*, tr. Mary Ann Koury Danner (Cambridge: Islamic Texts Society, 1996), pp. 43, 45.

it would indeed suffice for one who had penetrated to the heart of its meaning, a ruling which itself bears out the saying that the *Om mani padme hum* contains "the quintessence of the teaching of all the Buddhas". The fact that the Dalai Lama specifically exercises an "activity of presence" in this world in the name of the *Bodhisattva Chenrezig*,[83] revealer of *mani*, renders his comment in this instance all the more authoritative.'[84]

It is to be noted that Ibn 'Atā'Allāh proceeds to define this remembrance in the widest possible terms, and in doing so, enables us to see the extent to which the various forms of Buddhist devotion— including such practices as focusing upon the image of the Buddha or Bodhisattvas—can be incorporated within a broadly defined devotional category, 'the remembrance of God'. This makes it easier to see how forms of Buddhist devotion might be seen as akin to what would be regarded as authentic worship of the One by Muslims. Remembrance of God is defined by Ibn 'Atā'Allāh as 'the repetition of the Name of the Invoked by the heart and the tongue. It is alike whether it is God who is remembered, or one of His attributes, or one of His commandments, or one of His deeds ... Remembering God may take the form of a supplication to Him, or the remembrance of His Messengers, Prophets, saints or of anyone related to Him, or close to Him in some way, or because of some deed, such as reciting the Qur'ān, mentioning God's Name, poetry, singing, a conversation or a story.'[85]

The observations earlier regarding the deeper meaning of the 'Face' of God in the Qur'ān, together with al-Ghazālī's exegesis, help us to appreciate how it is that Ibn 'Atā'Allāh can include such practices as remembrance of God's Prophets and saints within the category of remembrance of God. For if God's Face is there, wherever one turns, one is, in principle, contemplating this Face, whatever be the immediate object of perception. However, in the case of ordinary objects, the 'face' which is ephemeral and illusory, pertaining to the object as such, casts a veil over the Face of God by means of which it derives its existence; the face of the relative eclipses the

---

83. This is the Tibetan name of Avalokiteshvara, the Bodhisattva of Compassion, referred to as Kwan-Yin in Chinese and Kwannon in Japanese, born of Amitābha (called Opagmed in Tibetan).

84. Marco Pallis, *A Buddhist Spectrum* (London: George Allen & Unwin, 1980), p. 89.

85. Ibid., p. 45.

Face of the Absolute. In the case of Prophets and saints, by contrast, given their effacement in the Face of the Absolute—their concrete realization that their own existence is, in Buddhist terms, 'empty'—this Face of the Absolute shines through their individuality. Thus, God is seen or remembered 'through' such saintly beings; for to use Buddhist terms again, it is the Absolute which 'exalts the holy persons' (*asamskrtaprabhāvitā hy ārya-pudgalā*).

This exalted spiritual station is referred to in the famous holy utterance (*hadīth qudsī*) in which God speaks in the first person on the tongue of the Prophet. Here, God declares 'war' on whosoever opposes one of His saints or more literally, 'friends' (*walī*, pl. *awliyā'*). Then follows this implicit description of the saint, who has devoted himself or herself entirely to God through supererogatory practices:

> My slave draws near to Me through nothing I love more than that which I have made obligatory for him. My slave never ceases to draw near to Me through supererogatory acts until I love him. And when I love him, I am his hearing by which he hears, his sight by which he sees, his hand by which he grasps, and his foot by which he walks.[86]

This passage of divine reality through the saint implies no compromise as regards divine transcendence. Quite to the contrary, for we are in the presence of the most radical manifestation of unsullied *tawhīd*, that oneness predicated upon complete integration: the saint, being one whose existence is effaced before God, allows free passage for divine transcendence to manifest through him/her as divine immanence; the sole reality of God, at once transcendent and immanent, inaccessible and yet inescapable, is affirmed in and through sanctity. The phenomenon of sanctity thus yields one of the most irrefutable proofs of *tawhīd*.

Allusion to this principle can be discerned in much of the devotional literature on the Prophet.[87] To take but one example, from the famous poem entitled *al-Burda*, of Imam al-Būsīrī: 'Truly, the bounty

---

86. See *An-Nawawī's Forty Hadith*, p. 118, no.38. It is cited there from Bukhārī, *Kitāb al-riqāq*, p. 992, no.2117.

87. One should always bear in mind that, in Islam, every prophet (*nabī*) is by definition a saint (*walī*), but not every saint is a prophet. Whatever is said about a saint applies equally to a prophet, who has all that the saint has, in addition to the specific function of prophecy. It should also be noted that the sanctity of the Prophet Muhammad is greater than that of any saint.

(*fadl*) of the Messenger of God has no limit, such that a speaker might be able to verbally articulate it'.[88] Only God's bounty, it might be argued, can be described as limitless; and yet, because the attribute of bounty manifested by the Prophet is not restricted by any egotistic appropriation on the part of the Prophet, that attribute must be seen as reverting ultimately or metaphysically to God. It pertains to God, as regards its uncreated essence, and to the Prophet, as regards its manifested form. The Prophet is described in the Qur'ān as 'kind and merciful' (*ra'ūf* and *rahīm*; see 9:128), qualities which are also used to describe God. The *Burda* mentions these and many other qualities of the Prophet, all of which are seen in the light of the duo-dimensionality noted above, both created and uncreated.

All of the virtues of the Prophet, without exception, are so many manifestations of qualities which in fact belong not to him but to God. In praising these qualities, one is praising God, while manifesting an intention to cultivate these qualities within oneself; the best way of cultivating them is emulating the *beautiful exemplar* (33:21), the Prophet in whom the human mode of those qualities were embodied to perfection. One is not reducing God to the level of the Prophet, rather, one is elevating to their divine source the qualities manifested by the Prophet, perceiving the transcendent archetypes of these qualities within the divine Essence.

Buddhist metaphysics helps us to see that what is being expressed here is far from the divinization of the Prophet, and thus a form of *shirk* (polytheism); rather, this mode of perceiving the prophetic qualities as expressions of their divine archetypes is demanded by a rigorous application of *tawhīd*. This perception will be all the more accurate and focused in the measure that one 'sees through' the Prophet; in other words, one sees that he is but a slave (*'abd*) or a 'poor one unto his Lord' (*faqīr ilā rabbihi*); thus, in Buddhist terms, he is one who is empty of himself (*svabhava*). The one who is most empty of his own self or *dharma* is the one who is most full of the *Dharma*: the pure, unsullied mirror of the Prophet's soul thus reflects God's Face; the praise directed initially to the character of the Prophet—the image of the Face reflected in the pure mirror—

---

88. As cited in the collection *Mukhkh al-'ibāda* (Beirut: Dār al-Hāwī, 2008), p. 552; see the excellent English translation of this poem by Shaykh Hamza Yusuf, *The Burda of al-Busiri* (Thaxted: Sandala, 2002). In his insightful introduction, Shaykh Hamza tells us that this poem 'is arguably the most memorized and recited poem in the Muslim world' (p. xvii).

is thus inevitably, and a fortiori, praise for the very nature of God—the Face as such, independent of the mirror reflecting it. It is in this way that remembrance of even a single attribute of the Prophet becomes remembrance of God, and thus rejoins the very purpose of all worship, which in turn is the purpose of creation: *I created the jinn and mankind only that they might worship Me* (51:56).[89]

Images of the Buddha, Blessings upon the Prophet

The citation above from Ibn 'Atā'Allāh, together with the *hadīth qudsī* describing the saint, helps one also to understand how it is that contemplation of the images of the Buddha—one of the central acts of devotion in the Buddhist tradition—can be regarded as a mode of 'remembrance of God'. For if it be accepted that the Buddha was one of the Messengers of God, and if remembrance of one of these Messengers is a form of remembrance of God, then the act of contemplation of the Buddha's image may be seen as a legitimate form of remembrance of God—especially given the fact that, unlike in Islam, there is no prohibition on the use of images in Buddhism. The vast kaleidoscopic universe of Buddhist iconography can thus be viewed not as a temptation to idolatry but as a form of remembrance. It is a form of devotion which passes through contemplation of the Buddha to remembrance of that ultimate Reality—the Dharma—which the Buddha had realized. The various forms of Buddhist contemplation are far from idolatrous fixations on the form of the Buddha; for this form is utterly 'empty'. The images which the devotee contemplates are described in the Tibetan Vajrayāna tradition as 'apparent but empty'.[90] The images 'appear' in this domain of manifestation, but they are transparent, allowing the devotee to see through them to the formless essence of which they are transient images—images which appear and thus, like all formal manifestation, disappear. Appearance implies disappearance, on the one hand; the manifested form implies the supra-manifest Essence, on the other. Such contemplation is in fact an invitation to contemplate, cultivate and assimilate the ultimate content of the enlightenment of the Buddha, and not simply to marvel at his superhuman beauty, although

---

89. According to Ibn 'Abbās—and following him, the majority of Qur'ānic commentators—the word *ya'budūni* ('they worship Me') here means: *ya'rifūni* ('they know Me').

90. See Reginald Ray, *Secret of the Vajra World* (Boston and London: Shambhala, 2002), p. 214.

this latter also has its part to play in the 'economy of salvation' as we shall see in a moment. In the words of Suzuki:

> The content of this enlightenment was explained by the Buddha as the Dharma which was to be directly perceived (*sanditthika*), beyond limits of time (*akalika*), to be personally experienced (*ehipassika*), altogether persuasive (*opanayika*), and to be understood each for himself by the wise (*paccattam veditabbo vinnuhi*).[91]

One of the most important teachers of the Pure Land doctrine in China, Tao-ch'o (d. 645), describes the four ways in which the Buddhas save:

1. Oral teachings, recorded and transmitted through books;
2. The 'supernatural beauty' of the Buddhas;
3. Their powers, virtues and transformations;
4. Their names.[92]

It can be argued that all four of these functions are performed by the Prophet in Islam. The 'oral teachings' are of course both 'his' as regards his own sayings (*hadīth*), but also God's as regards the Qur'ān and the 'holy utterances' (*ahādīth qudsiyya*). His beauty—one of the most remarked upon features in the devotional literature[93]—might not be regarded as 'salvific' in the strict sense, but it can be seen as cultivating a sense of the human perfection which he personified, and thus as enhancing devotional receptivity to the saving content of his message. As for his virtues, as seen above, they pertain not only to the realm of human character, but also to the divine source of all positive qualities: praising his virtues is a way not only of realizing those virtues within oneself, but is also a mode of praising God. It is thus not surprising to find that the Prophet said: 'I was sent *only* for

---

91. Suzuki, *Essays in Zen Buddhism*, op. cit., vol. 1, p. 61.

92. This is a quotation from a Sutra in Tao-ch'o's *Book of Peace and Happiness*; cited by Suzuki, *Essays in Zen Buddhism*, op. cit., vol. 2, p. 157.

93. On this subject see the fine essay by Mostafa Badawi, 'The Muhammadan Attributes' in *Seasons—Semiannual Journal of Zaytuna Institute Spring-Summer Reflections*, vol. 2, no.2, 2005, pp. 81–95. See also, for a general review of the literature on the subject of devotion to the Prophet, Annemarie Schimmel, *And Muhammad is His Messenger—The Veneration of the Prophet in Islamic Piety* (Chapel Hill and London: University of North Carolina Press, 1985), especially ch. 2 'Muhammad the Beautiful Model', pp. 24–55.

the sake of perfecting the most noble virtues' [94] (emphasis added). One might object: if perfecting virtue were the *sole* aim of the prophetic mission, what of praising God, prayer to God, remembrance of God, attaining salvation by these means? One simple answer is that the 'most noble virtues' include piety in its widest meaning: devotion, prayer, remembrance of God, and so forth. However, in light of our earlier discussion we could add this point also by way of reply: the *perfection* of virtues on the human plane is impossible without a total orientation to the divine source of all human virtues; then these virtues can be correctly grasped as so many mirrors reflecting the qualities of God. Each perfected virtue is then a mode of prayer, and rejoins the divine quality of which it is at once a reflection and a reminder. The Prophet, in whom and by whom all the noble virtues are perfected, is thus the most perfect mirror in which the utterly unknowable and eternally inaccessible Essence makes known and renders accessible Its own infinite perfections. As the Persian poet 'Abd al-Rahmān Jāmī (d. 1492) sings, addressing the Prophet:

> God made you the mirror of the Essence
> A looking-glass for the unique Essence. [95]

Finally, as regards the saving quality of the 'names' of the Buddha: we saw earlier that, in strict Buddhist logic, the name of the Buddha cannot be reduced to an appendage of the human Sakyamuni, for the name would then be no more real—in fact far less real—than the empirical substance of the sage himself: both name and named are alike 'empty of self'. The 'names' of the Buddha are thus to be seen as names of the eternal, absolute, transcendent attributes realized by Sakyamuni in his enlightenment. As we saw above, such a name as *Amitābha* saves not because it is an appendage (*nāma-rupa*) of the human being, Sakyamuni, but because it is one with the Named, the Reality designated by the Name: 'Infinite Light'.

What, therefore, can one say about the names of the Prophet? Among the most important names of the Prophet are *'Abd Allāh* (Slave of God) and *Dhikr Allāh*: these two names, alone, refer the devotee to the remembrance of God through the remembrance of the names of the Prophet. Given that he is a 'slave' of God, utterly empty of himself, all the human qualities manifest through him are likewise so many means of remembering God, as seen above. Joined

---

94. Cited in, among other sources, Ahmad b. Hanbal, 2:381.
95. Cited in Schimmel, op. cit., p. 131.

to this slavehood or emptiness, moreover, is the quality of remembrance. It is this utter receptivity to the Named which fills the void on the human plane. To invoke and praise the names of the Prophet is to praise the divine reality by which the Prophet's consciousness is penetrated: remembrance of the Prophet's names thus initiates an elevation of consciousness from these names to the names of God, and from these divine names to the Named (*al-musammā*), the Essence. To praise the Prophet is therefore also, and inescapably, to praise God, so that one can paraphrase the *shahāda* thus: 'No praised one (*hamīd*) but the Praised One (*al-Hamīd*)'.[96]

This way of looking at devotion to the Prophet provides an answer to critics within the Muslim tradition who claim that such devotion is a form of idolatry. It should be clear, however, that this form of devotion pertains to a subtle but rigorous and penetrating expression of *tawhīd*. This appreciation of *tawhīd* not only helps us to perceive the metaphysics underlying the practice of Buddhist contemplation of the image of the Buddha. It also helps us to perceive some of the deeper implications of the traditional Muslim practice of blessing the Prophet, a practice enjoined by the Qur'ān and defined by the Prophet himself. God instructs the believers: *Truly, God and His angels bless the Prophet; O ye who believe, bless him and greet him with peace* (33:56). Upon the revelation of this verse, the Prophet was asked how one was to perform this blessing, and he replied with this formula: 'O God, bless Muhammad and the descendents of Muhammad, as Thou hast blessed Abraham and the descendents of Abraham. Truly, thou art the Praised, the Glorious ...'[97] On the surface, this blessing, and its reward, is straightforward: each time one invokes this blessing upon the Prophet one receives ten blessings oneself—according to the Prophet. But at a deeper level, the invocation of blessings upon the Prophet can be understood to be a mode of praising God, for whatever blessing is received by a reflected image of the Essence reverts to the source of the image itself: one cannot bless the reflection of the Face without blessing the Face itself. Even the invocation of blessings upon the Prophet therefore passes through the Prophet and is received by God, who, in turn, showers blessings upon the soul of the devotee; in this way, blessing the Prophet and following in his footsteps is not just a mode of lov-

---

96. It is to be noted that the name Muhammad also means 'the praised one'.

97. This formula is then repeated almost verbatim, the word *sallī* ('bless') being replaced by a synonym, *bārik*.

76

ing God, it is also a magnet attracting God's love to oneself: *Say* [O Prophet]: *If you love God, follow me; God will love you* (3:31).

We are far from claiming that the Muslim and Buddhist forms of devotion to the Messenger/Buddha are identical, or reducible one to the other; rather, we are proposing that, however divergent be the forms taken by devotion to the founding figure of the respective traditions, it is possible to see these forms as expressions of principles which are analogous, if not identical: devotion to the human founder of the religions is a fundamental aspect and means of 'remembering God', in Islamic terms, or 'contemplating the *Dharma*' in Buddhist terms.

* * *

There is indeed for you in the Messenger of God a beautiful exemplar for those who place their hope in God and the Last Day, and who remember God much (33:21). This verse renders clear the relationship between following the Prophet and practising *dhikr Allāh*. Few, however, are able to follow the Prophetic *Sunna* in this domain, given that he was wont to spend long hours of each night in prayer:

> *Truly your Lord knows that you spend close to two-thirds of the night in prayer, and half of it, and a third of it—you and a group of those who are with you* (73:20)

This intensity of prayer was not aimed at something yet to be attained, rather, it flowed from sheer gratitude at what had been given, as is attested by the following incident. He was asked why he was standing in prayer at night, hour after hour, such that his feet swelled up, especially since he knew that God had 'forgiven' him any possible shortcomings on his part (referring to 48:1–2). The Prophet simply replied: 'Should I not be a grateful slave?'[98] What the Prophet did out of gratitude his followers are encouraged to do as a means of realizing that for the sake of which he was grateful: complete knowledge and unsurpassable virtue. The relationship between spiritual practice and the attainment of enlightenment is expressed in the verse: *Worship God until certainty comes to you* (15:99).[99] This reminds us of what Milarepa referred to as 'the most

---

98. Recounted in Qadi Iyad's *Ash-Shifā'*, tr. Aisha Abdarrahman Bewley, *Muhammad—Messenger of Allah* (Inverness: Madinah Press, 1991), p. 74.

99. The word translated as 'certainty' is *al-yaqīn*, which can be read also as 'the certain, i.e., death'. The two interpretations are complementary rather than contradictory, especially insofar as full enlightenment, hence absolute certainty, is predicated upon the spiritual 'death' which *fanā'* constitutes.

precious pith-instruction'. He calls his disciple, Gambopa, and offers it to him, saying, 'I only hope that you will cherish this teaching and never waste it. Now look!' Milarepa lifted up his robe to reveal a body covered with lumps and calluses, evidence of the intensity of his ascetic practices. Then he said: 'There is no profounder teaching than this. See what hardships I have undergone. The most profound teaching in Buddhism is *to practise*. It has simply been due to this persistent effort that I have earned the Merits and Accomplishment. You should also exert yourself perseveringly in meditation.' [100]

Although Islam does not permit any institutionalized form of monasticism, it certainly permits and encourages the kind of ascetic practice associated with the Prophetic Sunna. In both traditions, the intensity of worship is strongly encouraged, even if in Buddhism, a far greater stress is placed on ascetic practice as a form of teaching, and this is precisely on account of the supra-conceptual or even non-conceptual nature of Buddhist doctrines, which already intimate at their own non-essentiality, paradoxically exposing their own transparency, in order to precipitate a state of awareness which transcends all possible concepts. To quote Milarepa again:

> I practise the Dharma by heart and not by mouth ... I am ever happy for I never fall into the trap of mere conceptualization of the Void.[101]

---

100. *The Hundred Thousand Songs of Milarepa*, op. cit., p. 495.
101. Ibid., p. 377.

Part Three
Ethics of Detachment
and Compassion

In Islam there are no integral ethics that can be separated from one's quest for the 'Face' of God. The 'most pious', or the 'most mindful [of God]' (*al-atqā*) is described as one who *gives his wealth in order to purify himself; nobody possesses any good thing which might constitute a reward for this person—for he seeks only the Face of his Lord most High. And he, indeed, will be content* (92:18–21). Virtuous action generates this degree of contentment only if the action is motivated by the quest for God's good pleasure, without seeking any reward from those to whom one has been generous.[1] This intended orientation towards God is the dimension that adds spiritual depth and even a divine quality to those acts of human compassion and selfless generosity towards one's fellow human beings. Without that depth and quality, the acts remain good, no doubt, and there is a 'reward' for that goodness—*is the reward of beautiful goodness anything but beautiful goodness?* (55:60); but since these good acts are not fully integrated within the Sovereign Good (*al-Rahmān*), they cannot impart that serene contentment which is bestowed exclusively by the Sovereign Good upon those who think and act and live for its sake.

Can Buddhist ethics be seen by Muslims as predicated upon this quest for the Sovereign Good? The answer will be yes, if the arguments proffered above will be accepted—if, in other words, one accepts that the supreme goal in Buddhism corresponds closely to what is called the Essence of God in Islam. Since Buddhist ethics are clearly predicated upon the quest for the realization of the Absolute, we can thus assert that the ethical values shared in common by the two traditions are rooted in a quest for the Absolute, and should not be seen only within a framework of dialogue governed exclusively by the social domain.

Detachment: *Anicca* and *Zuhd*

It would be appropriate to begin this brief exploration of the shared ethical values between Buddhism and Islam by glancing at the ways

---

1. One should note that we have here one of the fundamental teachings of the *Bhagavad Gita*, referred to there as *nishkama karma*: acting while being detached from the fruits of one's actions.

in which we are to understand the nature of the world in which we live, according to the two traditions. Given the Buddhist conception of this world as being but one minute particle in the immeasurable series of universes of which the illusory web of *samsara* is woven, and given the Buddhist stress on the interminable series of reincarnations to which the unenlightened soul is susceptible within *samsara*, one might think that there is little in common between the two traditions as regards the fundamental attitude towards the 'world'. However, if one focuses upon the Buddhist idea of *anicca*, impermanence, and restricts one's view to the fundamental nature of this world—leaving out of account the cosmological framework within which this world is situated—then we will be brought to a position remarkably close to that fashioned by the Islamic understanding of 'the life of this world', *al-hayāt al-dunyā*.

Suffering

As was seen in the introduction, the crux of the Buddha's message concerns suffering and how to avoid it. The fact that we all undergo suffering (*dukkha*) is the first of the four 'noble truths'; the second is the cause of suffering: 'thirst' (*tanhā*, Sanskrit: *trishnā*) for the impermanent; the third is the cessation of suffering through the extinction of this thirst; and the fourth is the path that leads to the cessation of suffering. The crux of this fundamental teaching of the Buddha is the element of 'thirst'. This thirst for the perishable things of this world arises out of the ego in its unbridled, untamed, unmastered state. Not only does this thirst generate the seeds of suffering for oneself, by producing a passionate attachment to things from which one will ineluctably be detached, sooner or later; this thirst also gives rise to all the vices that result in the infliction of suffering upon others. Therefore, one must overcome thirst for the perishable both for the sake of one's liberation from suffering, and for the sake of liberating others from the consequences of one's egotistically-driven vices. The opposite of suffering is not simply a state of ease for the ego; it is the highest good—*Nirvana*, thus, the Absolute, which transcends the ego and all its states. Thus the fundamental motivation for ridding oneself of suffering is not situated on the same plane as that upon which the suffering is located—the empirical ego. For this ego is, like all compounded (*samskrta*) things, itself impermanent, whence the idea of *anattā* or no-self. Rather, the motivation for this liberation from suffering is grounded in a quest for the Dharma, the Buddha-nature; in other words, it is grounded in that which is incommensurable with the ego. Thus, when one speaks of the ethical actions called for by the 'eightfold path'—this path being the detailed expression of the fourth noble truth, viz., the path to the cessation of suffering—one is speaking about a quest that is more than simply ethical, and more than simply the cessation of suffering for the individual. Rather, this quest is for what in Islam is called the 'Face of God'. The ethical necessity of overcoming egotism thus rejoins and is deepened by the spiritual imperative of transcending the ego for the sake of the Absolute.

Ridding oneself of thirst for the impermanent, then, is of the highest significance both in ethical and in spiritual terms. Such cardinal virtues as generosity and compassion, kindness and humility, patience and forbearance, arise in the measure of one's success in rupturing the symbiotic nexus between egotism and the things of this world, between a false subject and the multitude of false objects. Overcoming egotism, the source of all the vices, requires depriving it of its life-blood, and this life-blood of egotism is 'thirst'; overcoming 'thirst' requires in its turn a concrete apprehension of the impermanence of all those things which can be thirsted after. Thus, a correct understanding of *anicca* lies at the heart of that ethical imperative: overcoming egotism.

As noted in the introduction, one key element of a recurring description of those who are saved in the Hereafter relates to suffering. As seen in 2:62, *whoever believes in God and the Last Day and performs virtuous acts—for such, their reward is with their Lord, no fear or grief will befall them.* One should note that *huzn*, sadness or grief, is absent from the souls of the saved, in the Hereafter, and, for the sanctified, in this world. For the *awliyā'*, the saints, or 'friends' of God, are described in these very terms, in their present state, in this world:

> *Indeed, as for the friends of God, they have no fear nor do they grieve—those who believe and are mindful. Theirs are good tidings in this world and in the Hereafter...*(10:62–64).

Whereas for ordinary believers, the 'good tidings' pertain to the Hereafter, the saints are given the same good tidings in this world; for, here and now, they have achieved that state of contentment with God, and detachment from the world. The word 'mindful' translates *yattaqūn*, which derives from a root meaning 'to guard' or 'protect' oneself: the implication is that one guards oneself from the punishment of God by avoiding evil and doing good, in full awareness of God's inescapable presence. The key term, *taqwā*, is thus often translated as 'piety' or 'God-consciousness', but it can equally well be translated as 'mindfulness' a term so closely associated with Buddhist ethics. Those who are 'mindful' of God are, by that very token, 'guarding' themselves against the perils of attachment to the 'life of the world', *al-ḥayāt al-dunyā*. They are guarding themselves against that which the Prophet warned his followers about most solemnly: 'I do not fear that you will fall into idolatry (*shirk*), but I do fear that you will fall for this world—aspiring for it in competition with each other.'[2]

Worldliness

It would be well to note some more sayings of the Prophet in connection with the pitfalls of worldliness, sayings which reinforce this resonance between the Muslim and Buddhist conception of the impermanence of this world:

Be in this world as if you were a stranger or a wayfarer.[3]

The heart of an old man remains young in two respects: his love of this world and his far-fetched hopes.[4]

If the son of Adam [i.e., the human being] had two valleys full of money, he would desire a third, for nothing can fill the belly of the son of Adam except dust.[5]

The fire of hell is veiled by passionate desires, while Paradise is veiled by undesirable things.[6]

Remember much that which ends all pleasures (*hādhim al-ladhdhāt*): Death.[7]

Death is a precious gift to the believer.[8]

2. *Saḥīḥ al-Bukhārī*, tr. M.M. Khan (Chicago: Kazi Publications, 1977), vol. 2, p. 239, no. 428.

3. Bukhārī (Summarised), tr. M.M. Khan (Riyadh: Makataba Dar-us-Salam, 1994), p. 981, no. 2092 (translation modified).

4. Ibid., pp. 982–983, no. 2096 (translation modified).

5. Ibid., p. 984, no.2100.

6. Ibid., p. 989, no.2110 (translation modified).

7. Tirmidhī, *Qiyāma*, 26; and Nasā'ī, *Janā'iz*, 3, as cited by T.J. Winter (tr. & ed.), *Al-Ghazālī—The Remembrance of Death and the Afterlife* (Cambridge: Islamic Texts Society, 1989), p. 9.

8. Ibid., p. 9. The saying is found in Hākim, iv.319; and Tabarānī's *al-Mu'jam al-kabīr* (Haythamī, *Majma'* II.320; X.309), as per Winter's note 13, p. 262.

It is thus not surprising that the Prophet also said: 'Die before you die.'[9]

Taken together, these sayings emphasise not just the imperative of detachment or *zuhd* in relation to the false plenitude of the world, they also underscore the link between dying to the ego and dying to the world: one has to rupture the symbiotic relationship between the inner subjective pole of egotism and the outer objective pole of things. This spiritual imperative is also affirmed in the Qur'ān in ways which are both strikingly obvious and, as we shall see, extremely subtle. This same link between the inner pole of egotism and the outer attraction of things is underlined in the *Sutta Nipata* in the following very important passage, which might indeed be read as a commentary on the prophetic injunction: die before you die.

> Short indeed is this life. This side of a hundred years it perishes. And even if one live beyond, yet of decay he perishes at last. It is from selfishness that people grieve. "Not lasting are possessions in this world: all this is liable to change"—so seeing, let not a man stay in his house [i.e., cling to self].[10] By death is put away even that of which one thinks, "This is mine own". So seeing, let not one devote himself to selfishness. As, when one awakes, he sees no more him whom he met in a dream, even so, one sees no more the beloved one who hath died, and become a ghost.[11]

In this short passage the relationship between the principle of impermanence and the vice of selfishness is well defined. He who fails to comprehend the existential fatality of death cannot transcend his own equally fatal egotism: selfishness 'kills' all virtue just as surely as the compounded, originated nature of all things ensures their extinction:

> Impermanent, alas, are all compounded things. Their nature is to rise and fall. When they have risen, they cease. The bringing of them to an end is bliss.[12]

---

9. Tirmidhī, *Qiyāma*, 25.

10. The 'house' symbolises the self, as can be seen in the following saying from the Dhammapada (verse 154, p. 56–57): 'But now, I have seen thee, housebuilder: never more shalt thou build this house. The rafters of sin are broken. The ridge-pole of ignorance is destroyed. The fever of craving is past: for my mortal mind is gone to the joy of the immortal Nirvana.'

11. *Sutta Nipata*, v. 804–807—cited on p. 187 of *Some Sayings*.

12. *Digha Nikāya*, II., 198, cited on p. 188 of *Some Sayings*.

Mara, the principle of death for the outer world of things, is also the source of all temptation and sin for the inner world of the soul; the following sayings heighten our awareness of this inner nexus between ignorance, egotism and sin: that is, the mutually reinforcing relationships between deficiency on the plane of knowledge, susceptibility to delusion on the plane of psychology, and the propensity to evil on the plane of morality:

> Who shall conquer this world ... and the world of Yama,[13] of death and of pain? ... He who knows that this body is the foam of a wave, the shadow of a mirage, he breaks the sharp arrows of Mara, concealed in the flowers of sensuous passions and, unseen by the King of Death, he goes on and follows his path.[14]

> When a man considers this world as a bubble of froth, and as the illusion of an appearance, then the king of death has no power over him.[15]

Subtle Polytheism

These subtle relationships and causal connections are the life-blood of the suffering which flows from the impermanence of all things; they point to the condition of 'mutual arising' or 'interdependent causation' (*pratītyasamutpāda*) which characterizes the outer world, and attachment to which generates suffering in the soul. This key psychological insight into the human condition is of immense practical value in terms of Buddhist-Muslim dialogue, if the aim of such dialogue is to go beyond merely establishing formal resemblances as regards ethical teachings on the plane of social relations and give rise, instead, to a process of mutual illumination on the level of spiritual insight into the human condition. More specifically, the acute and penetrating insights fashioned by the Buddhist stress on *anicca* can help Muslims bring into sharper focus those teachings within the Qur'ān and the Sunna which pertain to the necessity of *zuhd* or detachment with regard to the world. These teachings can be divided into two categories, overt, relating to the evanescence of the 'life of this world', and subtle, relating to a complex and calibrated apprehension of the meaning of idolatry and disbelief.

---

13. Yama is the guardian of hell in Buddhist cosmology.
14. *Dhammapada*, 44 and 46, p. 42.
15. *Dhammapada*, 170, p. 60

On the overt plane, we can observe clear parallels with the Buddhist teaching of impermanence. For example, in the *Dhammapada* we read:

> The wise do not call a strong fetter that which is made of iron, of wood or of rope; much stronger is the fetter of passion for gold and for jewels, for sons or for wives.[16]

This is clearly echoed in such verses of the Qur'ān as the following:

> *Know that the life of the world is only play, and idle talk, and pomp, and boasting between you, and rivalry in wealth and children; as the likeness of vegetation after rain, whose growth is pleasing to the farmer, but afterwards it dries up and you see it turning yellow, then it becomes straw...* (57:20)

The Buddhist reference to the world as 'a bubble of froth' (*Dhammapada*, 170 cited above) evokes the following Qur'ānic image:

> *He sends down the water from the sky, so that valleys flow according to their measure, and the flood bears swelling foam—from that which they smelt in the fire in order to make ornaments and tools, there rises a foam like it—thus does God strike* [a similitude to distinguish] *the true and the false. Then as for the foam, it passes away as scum upon the banks, while as for that which is useful to mankind, it remains in the earth* (13:17).

Turning to the more subtle type of Qur'ānic teaching, let us note that these teachings are brought into sharper focus by the Buddhist perspective on impermanence. More specifically, the deeper meanings and implications of such cardinal vices are rendered clearer in the light of the Buddhist stress on the way in which ignorance of impermanence, as seed, produces attachment to the ego, with all the vices that result from such egotism, as its fruit. As seen above in the *Sutta Nipata*, v. 804–807, one no longer resides in the 'house' of one's ego as soon as one grasps that everything that one apparently possesses will be taken away:

> By death is put away even that of which one thinks, 'This is mine own'. So seeing, let not one devote himself to selfishness.

---

16. *Dhammapada*, 345, p. 84.

One observes a subtle allusion to this deluded condition in several passages of the Qur'ān; indeed, in the one which we shall look at below, the condition in question is described in terms of the cardinal sins of *shirk* (idolatry) and *kufr* (disbelief). These sins are ascribed to those who are formally defined as 'believers'. We thus come to see that these sins, far from being exhausted by their literal, overt dimensions, in fact refer to subtle and complex psychological states so clearly highlighted in the Buddhist perspective.

This is a passage from the chapter entitled 'The Cave' (*al-Kahf*, 18:32–42):

Coin for them a similitude: Two men, unto one of whom We had assigned two gardens of grapes, and We had surrounded both with date-palms and had put between them tillage. / Each of the gardens gave its fruit and withheld nothing. And We caused a river to gush forth therein. / And he had fruit. And he said unto his comrade, when he spoke with him: I am more than you in wealth, and stronger in respect of men. / And he went into his garden, thus wronging himself. He said: I do not think that all this will ever perish. / I do not think that the Hour will ever come; and if indeed I am brought back to my Lord, I surely shall find better than this as a resort. / His comrade, when he spoke with him, exclaimed: Do you disbelieve in Him Who created you of dust, then of a drop, and then fashioned you a man? / But He is God, my Lord, and I ascribe unto my Lord no partner. / If only, when you had entered your garden, you had said: That which God wills [will come to pass]! *There is no strength save in God! Though you regard me as less than you in wealth and children, / Yet it may be that my Lord will give me something better than your garden, and will send on it a bolt from heaven, and some morning it will be a smooth hillside, / Or some morning its water will be lost in the earth so that you cannot search for it. / And his fruit was beset* [with destruction]. *Then he began to wring his hands for all that he had spent upon it, when (now) it was all ruined on its trellises, and to say: Would that I had ascribed no partner to my Lord!*

What is to be noted here is that the proud and boastful owner of the orchards is a believer in God, at least overtly and formally: he believes in his 'Lord', he speaks of returning to his Lord, and is aware, at some level at least, that the Hour—the end of his life, and that of the cosmos, the Day of Judgement and then eternity—is a reality that cannot be evaded; he believes, though, that even if he is 'returned' to God, he will receive something even more satisfying 'as a resort'. Yet, despite his knowledge and apparent faith in God, his attitudes are described in terms of idolatry and disbelief: he falls into *shirk* and *kufr* because of his ignorance of the impermanence, and ultimately illusory nature, of 'his' possessions. His comrade, a humble believer, remonstrates with him not in relation to his pride and his boasting, but in relation to his subtle *disbelief*: *Do you disbelieve in Him Who created you of dust, then of a drop, and then fashioned you a man?* The vices of boastfulness and exultation in one's possessions are here grasped at their root, as manifestations of *kufr*, and not just *kibr* (pride). For his part, the true believer affirms: *But He is God, my Lord, and I ascribe unto my Lord no partner.* The strong implication here is this: *your* attitude, by contrast, not only manifests disbelief in God, it also implies that you ascribe unto God a partner, thus becoming a *mushrik*, a polytheist. These implications are confirmed by the words of the owner of the gardens, after he sees them ruined: *Would that I had ascribed no partner to my Lord!*

The 'god' of Desire

Disbelief in God and ascribing partners to Him, therefore, are not simply questions of denying His existence and overtly setting up some stones and statues to worship instead of Him. Rather, one can delude oneself into thinking that one is a true believer, on the basis of some purely mental or verbal attestation of belief, while in fact being dominated by states of mind and being which belie that belief, and which indeed belie one's religion, even if one is accomplishing its formal rites. This is the message which is given in the following short chapter of the Qur'ān, entitled 'Small Kindnesses' (*al-Māʿūn*, 107:1–7):

> *Have you observed him who belies religion?*
> *That is the one who repels the orphan,*
> *And urges not the feeding of the poor.*

So woe unto worshippers,
Who are heedless of their prayer;
Who would be seen [at worship],
Yet refuse small kindnesses!

This is more than simply a question of religious hypocrisy, overtly believing in Islam, while secretly disbelieving in it. Rather, one can see that these worshippers may indeed be convinced of Islam at the level of belief and outward action, while *de facto* violating its spiritual substance by their vice of miserliness, which manifests their egotism: it is this egotism which effectively takes the place of God as the actual, existential source of their inmost motivation: *Have you seen him who makes his desire (hawā) his god?* (25:43; almost identical at 45:23). The sense of the 'I' eclipses the light of divine guidance. One may even make great exertions for the sake of God and religion, but be bound by this hidden idolatry of the self. One sees a clear parallel here with the teachings of Buddhism. In addition to what we have observed earlier, let us note here the compelling verses of Milarepa, showing how impossible it is to free oneself from oneself if the sense of self be predominant:

He who strives for Liberation with
The thought of 'I' will ne'er attain it.
He who tries to loosen his mind-knots
When his spirit is neither great nor free,
Will but become more tense.[17]

Milarepa also expresses a theme which resonates strongly with Muslim ethics in the following verses:

To give charity without compassion
Is like tying oneself to a pillar
With a strong leather strap;
It only binds one tighter [in Samsara's prison].[18]

The Qur'ān's teaching on charity is similar: *A kind word with forgiveness is better than almsgiving followed by injury* (2:263).
Now, returning to the boastful owner of the gardens, one sees that this egoistic motivation and orientation is given expression in his two statements: first, he boasts to his neighbor, *I am more than you*

17. *The Hundred Thousand Songs of Milarepa* (tr. Garma C.C. Chang) (Shambhala: Boston & Shaftsbury, 1989), vol. 2, p. 524.
18. Ibid., vol. 2, p. 559.

in wealth, and stronger in respect of men. Having engaged in this delusion of grandeur and the belittling of his neighbor, this demonstration of egotism and pride is then followed by an expression of the secret source which feeds that egotism and pride. The words he speaks in this parable give voice to the mental insinuations and worldly orientations to which the soul is subject, even the soul of the believer: *I do not think that all this will ever perish.* This failure to register the impermanence of 'all this' goes to the root of his *de facto* state of disbelief, one which is moreover compounded by idolatry: not only is he guilty of setting up partners to God in the form of his wealth, which he deems to be imperishable, and thus eternal; but also, he sets up as god his own *hawā*, the desire, whim, caprice, of his own soul. There is a symbiosis between one's 'desire' elevated as god, on the one hand, and belief in the imperishability of one's possessions in the world, on the other:

> *Woe unto every slandering traducer, he who has gathered wealth and counts it; he believes that his wealth will render him immortal* (104:1–3).

The Qur'ān sums up the essence of salvation in terms of a polarity, one pole of which is positive, the other negative; the former defined in terms of God and the latter in terms of *hawā*: *But as for the one who fears the station of his Lord, and restrains his soul from its* hawā, *verily the Garden will be his abode* (79:40–41). The false god of one's *hawā* is reined in and overcome in the very measure that one's concern is with the one and only true God. Conversely, if one's *hawā* is the actual source of one's motivation, then one falls into subtle idolatry, even if belief in God is affirmed at the formal level.

One only has to substitute the word 'thirst' (*tanhā*) for 'desire' (*hawā*) to see the similarities between the teachings of Buddhism and the Qur'ān on the imperative of transcending the appetites of the lower soul. The Buddhist perspective—in so rigorously negating the idea of the ultimate reality of the individual soul (*anattā*), in so sharply focusing upon the craving that is the source of all suffering, and in so strongly stressing the impermanence (*anicca*) of all objects of craving in this world—can help the Muslim to discern a very similar teaching in the Qur'ān. One comes to divinize oneself through elevation of one's 'desire' to the implicit status of divinity; this being an attitude which is fed by the delusion of the permanence of worldly possessions; and this in turn is fed by the desire of the ego to aggrandize itself at the expense of others. The resulting egotism ensures that the vices of pride and miserliness will be manifested instead of humility and generosity. It is not just worldly possessions that, being seen as imperishable, feed the implicit *kufr* and *shirk* of the soul; rather, these vices are fed by every single relativity to which one consciously or subconsciously attaches an absolute significance. Everything pertaining either to the world or to the ego, such as bodily satisfactions, desire for acknowledgement, thirst for praise, and even spiritual attainments: as soon as these elements are given disproportionate attention and importance, then one falls into the subtle forms of *kufr* and *shirk* highlighted in the Qur'ānic parable. One sees the deeper meaning of the verse: *Most of them believe not in God, without being idolators* (12:106). Only the utterly sincere believers—referred to as those made pure, or rendered sincere (*mukhlas*) by God—are capable of avoiding the pitfalls of subtle worldliness which are tantamount to covert *shirk*. In verse 38:83, Satan declares that he will 'beguile' every single soul, 'except Your purified slaves' (*mukhlasūn*). Satan is also instructed by God to be a 'partner' with human beings in their worldly goods and their children: ... *and be a partner in their wealth and children, and promise them: Satan promises only to beguile* (17:64). For this reason, perhaps, we are told to see in our own wealth and children so many 'temptations' (*fitna*) (7:27); and that within our wives and children there are 'enemies' (64:14). The fundamental reason why one must beware of them is given in the following verse: *O you who believe, let not your wealth nor your children distract you from the remembrance of God, Those who do, they are the losers* (63:9). The remembrance of God is the best antidote to the poison of worldly attachment.

Mention was made above of even 'spiritual goods' being a possible source of subtle attachment and thus of *shirk*. Again, the Buddhist perspective helps the Muslim to become sensitive to the deeper implications contained in the parable we have been considering. The 'gardens' in the parable can also be understood as metaphors for spiritual fruits, cultivated by prayer, meditation and ascetic discipline: the proud possessor of these fruits pretentiously believes that he will not be subject to Judgement, but will rather be elevated into a greater Garden of Paradise, of which his earthly garden of spiritual fruit is a foretaste. This state of mind describes what has been aptly referred to as 'spiritual materialism' in the Buddhist tradition.[19] In the *Udumbarika Sihanāda Sutta* the Buddha alerts his followers to the pitfalls of pride and ostentation which lie in wait for the recluse who engages in intense ascetic discipline.[20] The Buddha was confronted by just such ostensibly 'spiritual' attitudes amongst the various pretenders to religious authority in his time. Believing that they had attained sanctity and deliverance in their life-times, deluded 'eternalists' ascribed eternity and thus divinity to their relative, transient souls, on account of the mystical powers and states they had mastered. The combined power of the doctrines of *anicca* and *anattā* dialectically exposed the hollowness of the claim to possess a soul which was at one and the same time individual and eternal.[21] Only the *Dharma, Nirvana, Shūnya*—or the Essence of God, in Islamic terms—is absolute, eternal and infinite; all else is transient, and thirst for the transient is the seed of suffering, as well as being the fruit of delusion.

The proud possessor of the gardens in our parable can thus be seen to represent the deepest source of this kind of delusion, and not just the obvious manifestation of the delusion in the form of pride and boastfulness. This interpretation of the parable is lent support by the fact that immediately following the parable come these words: *In this case is* al-walāya *only from God, the True...* (18:44). The word *walāya* here is conventionally understood in the sense of 'protection', in accordance with the context of the literal meaning of the parable: there is no protection against destruction of one's goods except from God. But *walāya* can also be understood to mean 'sanctity', in accordance with this deeper interpretation of the parable, which can be read as a reminder to all would-be saints that their spiritual attainments are of no significance unless these attainments lead to self-effacement and not self-glorification: one is to be effaced in the divine source of all sanctity, and not elevated through claiming possession of that sanc-

---

19. See Chogyam Trungpa, *Cutting Through Spiritual Materialism* (Boston: Shambhala, 1973).

20. As cited by Elizabeth J. Harris, *Detachment and Compassion in Early Buddhism* (Kandy, Sri Lanka: Buddhist Publication Society, 1997), p. 4.

21. It has been claimed that the Buddha did not come into contact with any realized master of the Upanishads, who understood the necessity of upholding the transcendence of *Paramātman* (supreme Atman, or Brahma Nirguna, Brahma 'beyond qualities') vis-á-vis the *jīvātman* (the individual soul within which Atman immanent within the individual soul). See Ananda Coomaraswamy, *Buddha and the Gospel of Buddhism*, op. cit., p. 199.

tity as one's own. In Buddhist terms, such a claim would be a form of 'grasping' (*upādāna*), and more specifically, *attavādupādāna*: grasping at a particular idea of the self,[22] in this case, the idea that one's self has achieved authenticity and realization through becoming adorned by the fruits of one's spiritual endeavours: if *I do not think that all this will ever perish*, then the self which possesses 'all this', will likewise be deemed to be imperishable.

This section can be brought to a fitting end with the penetrating words of the Shin Buddhist already cited above, Kenryo Kanamatsu, which will surely resonate with any Muslim sensitive to the need for *zuhd* in relation to the 'life of the world': 'All our belongings assume a weight by the ceaseless gravitation of our selfish desires; we cannot easily cast them away from us. They seem to belong to our very nature, to stick to us as a second skin, and we bleed as we detach them.'[23]

Loving Compassion: *Karunā* and *Rahma*

Compassion, even on the human plane, is not just a sentiment, it is an existential quality. This existential quality presupposes a concrete sense of participation in the suffering of others, as is expressed by the etymology of the word: com-passion means to 'suffer with' another. The metaphysics of unity finds its most appropriate ethical expression in this quality, for when the illusion of separation is overcome, the suffering of the other becomes one's own, and the virtues of compassion and mercy, generosity and love become the hallmarks of the character of one who has truly realized Unity. Similarly, as seen in the previous section, when self-preoccupation is overcome, together with the worldliness, subtle or overt, which feeds it, then the same qualities centered on compassionate love will flow forth naturally and spontaneously: these qualities, inherent in the spiritual substance or *fitra* of each soul, will no longer be constrained or suffocated by coagulations of egotism and worldliness. Rather, compassionate love will emanate to the whole of creation, the compassionate soul will reflect and radiate the all-encompassing grace of God. Speaking of two types, those who reject God and those who believe in Him, the Qur'ān declares:

---

22. This is the ultimate form taken by 'grasping', the other three consist of *kāmupādāna*: grasping of sense-pleasures; *ditthūpādāna*, grasping of views; *silabbatupādāna*, grasping of rules, precepts or customs.

23. Kenryo Kanamatsu, *Naturalness*, op. cit., p. 7.

Unto each, the former and the latter, do We extend the gracious gift of thy Lord. And the gracious gift of thy Lord can never be confined behind walls (17:20).

This is because God's *Rahma*, being infinite, can be excluded from nowhere, from nobody: *My loving Compassion encompasses all things* (7:156).

Islam and Buddhism come together on the centrality of this quality of compassionate love, and for both traditions, this human quality is inseparable from the Absolute, in which it is rooted, and to which it leads. In this section we hope to show that the Islamic conception of *Rahma* makes explicit what is largely implicit in the earliest texts of the Pali canon; in this respect, it can be seen to serve a function similar to that of Mahayana Buddhism, wherein compassion comes to play a determinative role, elevated as the very principle, cosmological and not simply ethical, which motivates the *Buddhas* and *Bodhisattvas*. We would therefore argue that for both Muslims and Buddhists, the quality of loving compassion must determine the core of one's personality, and it must dominate the nature of one's conduct in relation to others; this ideal, at once ethical and spiritual, derives its ultimate justification and transformative power from the fact that it expresses on the human plane a principle which is rooted in the heart of the Absolute.

As is well known, in Islam one consecrates every action, and not just ritual action, with the *basmala*—that is, the formula *Bismillāh al-Rahmān al-Rahīm*, in the Name of God, the Lovingly Compassionate, the Lovingly Merciful. It is entirely appropriate that all initiative should begin with the 'names of mercy', for it is merciful love which lies at the very root of creation in Islam, as will be seen below. In both traditions compassion is inseparable from love, *mettā* in Buddhism[24] and *mahabba* in Islam. In Buddhism one even finds the compound *maitrī-karunā* 'love-compassion' which expresses the intertwining of these two principles; in Islam, likewise, *Rahma* cannot be adequately translated by the single English word 'compassion' or 'mercy',

---

24. *Anukampā* and *dayā*, translated as 'sympathy', are closely related to the idea of compassion. See Harvey Aronson, *Love and Sympathy in Theravada Buddhism* (Delhi: Motilal Banarsidass, 1980), p. 11. As Reverend Tetsuo Unno notes in his introduction to Kanamatsu's *Naturalness* (p. xiii), the author uses the English word 'love' to translate *karunā*, normally translated as 'compassion'.

but requires the addition of the element of love.[25]

A compelling reason for translating *Rahma* as loving compassion and not just compassion—and certainly not just 'mercy'—is provided by the Prophet's use of this word in the following incident. At the conquest of Mecca, certain captives were brought to the Prophet. There was a woman among them, running frantically and calling for her baby; she found him, held him to her breast and fed him. The Prophet said to his companions: 'Do you think this woman would cast her child into the fire?' We said, 'No, she could not do such a thing.' He said, 'God is more lovingly compassionate (*arham*) to His servants than is this woman to her child.'[26] The *Rahma* of God is here defined by reference to a quality which all can recognize as love: the mother's acts of compassion and mercy stream forth from an overwhelming inner love for her child. One cannot love another without feeling compassionate to that person, while one can feel compassion for someone without necessarily loving that person.

The Jewish scholar Ben-Shemesh goes so far as to translate the *basmala* as 'In the Name of God, the Compassionate, the Beloved' to bring home this key aspect of love proper to the root of *Rahma*.[27] He argues that in both Arabic and Hebrew the meaning of love is strongly present in the root *r-h-m*, and gives the following evidence: Psalm number 18 contains the phrase: *Erhamha Adonay*—'I love thee my Lord'.[28] In Aramaic/Syriac, the root *r-h-m* specifically denotes love, rather than 'compassion'. One can thus feel the resonance of this Syriac connotation within the Arabic *Rahma*. Moreover, there is epigraphic evidence that early Christian sects in southern Arabic used the name *Rahmānan* as a name of God, and this would probably have been understood as 'The Loving'.[29]

God's *Rahma* is described by the Prophet as being greater than that of the woman for her child, implying that the transcendent proto-

---

25. See our essay 'God "The Loving"', in Miroslav Volf, Ghazi bin Muhammad, Melissa Yarrington (eds.), *A Common Word—Muslims and Christians on Loving God and Neighbor* (Grand Rapids, Michigan/Cambridge UK: William B. Eerdmans, 2010).

26. Bukhārī, *Sahīh, kitāb al-adab, bāb* 18 *hadīth* no. 5999 (Bukhari summarized: p. 954, no. 2014); Muslim, *Sahīh, kitāb al-tawba, hadīth* no. 6978.

27. See A. Ben Shemesh, 'Some Suggestions to Qur'ān Translators', in *Arabica*, vol. 16, no. 1, 1969, p. 82.

28. Ibid.

29. See Albert Jamme, 'Inscriptions on the Sabaean Bronze Horse of the Dumbarton Oaks Collection', in *Dumbarton Oaks Papers*, vol. 8 (1954), pp. 323–324 et passim.

type of this most loving and compassionate of all human qualities is found in the divine Reality. Before examining this question any further, it is interesting to note that the Buddha refers to an almost identical image in order to bring home the meaning of *mettā*, the love that is inseparable from *karunā*. This is from a passage in the *Mettā-sutta* ('Teaching on love') in the Pali canon:

> Even as a mother watches over and protects her child, her only child, so with a boundless mind should one cherish all living beings, radiating friendliness over the entire world, above, below, and all around without limit. So let him cultivate a boundless good will towards the entire world, uncramped, free from ill will or enmity. Standing or walking, sitting or lying down, during all his waking hours, let him establish this mindfulness of good will, which men call the highest state![30]

It is out of compassion, indeed, that the Buddha preached his *Dhamma*: his desire was to liberate people from suffering by enlightening them as to its cause, and showing them the path to eliminate that cause. It is clear, then, that even in early Buddhism compassion was not just a cardinal virtue, it went to the very heart of the Buddhist *upāya*, 'expedient means' or 'saving strategy.' However, it is to be noted that the Mahayana stress on compassion goes well beyond anything found in Hinayāna texts. In the latter, compassion remains fundamental and indispensable, but in Mahayana texts, it takes on altogether mythological[31] dimensions, and enters into the definition of what most closely approximates the Personal God in Buddhism, namely, the Buddha of Infinite Light, *Amitābha*. By tracing the compassionate function of Gautama the sage back to its principial root, Mahayana Buddhism helps to solve a logical problem within the very structure of Theravada Buddhism, or at least makes explicit what is implicit in the earlier tradition. The logical problem is this: If there is no individual soul who suffers, what is the entity that can be said to receive compassion, and whence comes this compassion if the soul of the one imparting it is likewise non-existent—if the compassionate soul is but a conglomeration of empirical and psychic envelopes (*skandha*s), with no essential reality? Given the fact that survival after death, in heavens and hells, is clearly indicated by the

---

30. E. Conze, *Buddhist Scriptures* (Baltimore, 1968), p. 186.
31. See note 65, Chapter 1, regarding the root-meaning of myth.

Buddha, one has to conclude that something akin to a soul does in fact persist posthumously, and it is this 'something' which can either be elevated to the heavens or reduced to the hells, according to the degree to which it assimilates the teachings and acts according to the dictates of the compassionate wisdom of the Buddha.

Source of Compassion

But this leaves out of account the question: what is the ultimate source of the compassion of the Buddha? A simple answer would be that this source is none other than the enlightened state itself: compassion flows forth from the very nature of Nirvana or *Shūnya*. But the question remains: how does compassion spring forth from an *impersonal* or supra-personal state, when the very nature of compassion is so clearly *personal*, that is, it so intimately implies a personal will, actively and compassionately involved in the lives of suffering humanity, a personal will which, moreover, must at the same time be transcendent or absolute. It must be transcendent, otherwise it could not save relative beings through its compassion; but it must also assume a dimension of relativity, otherwise it would have no relation to living human beings. It is precisely this combination of absolute transcendence and personal compassion which is expressed in the Islamic conception of God's *Rahma* and in the various heavenly Buddhas depicted in later Mahayana texts.[32]

The principle of compassion, so perfectly embodied in Gautama the sage, infinitely transcended his own empirical individuality. As cited earlier: 'Those who by my form did see me, and those who followed me by my voice, wrong are the efforts they engaged in; me those people will not see. From the Dharma one should see the Buddha, for the dharma-bodies are the guides.'[33] The compassion proper to the *Dharma* is universal; Gautama the sage manifested this quality in one particular modality. This relationship between the particular and the universal is expressed in Buddhism by means of the mythology of cosmic Buddhas existing in unimaginably distant aeons prior to the earthly appearance of the Gautama. Mahayana

---

32. This celestial level of the manifestation of the Buddha-principle being referred to as *Sambhoga-kāya*, in contradistinction to the *Dharma-kāya*—which, as noted earlier, pertains to the supra-manifest Essence—and the *Nirmāna-kāya*, the human form of the earthly Buddha.

33. *Vajracchedikā*, 26a, b. Cited in *Buddhist Texts Through the Ages*, op. cit., p. 144.

texts therefore present a picture of a 'Personal God' with diverse traits—the *Ādi-Buddha*, *Vairochana*, *Amitābha*, etc—without whose grace and mercy, one cannot attain salvation into the 'Pure Land', let alone that state of *Nirvana* wherein the various Buddhas are all transcended. It is clear that Mahayana Buddhism comes close to the Islamic conception of divinity as regards the root of the quality of compassion, and both make explicit a metaphysically irrefutable principle, one about which the Buddha himself was silent, but which he did not contradict: compassion cannot be exhausted by its purely human manifestation; on the contrary, it derives all its power and efficacy from its supra-human, absolute or 'divine' source. This source is transcendent, but insofar as it radiates towards all creatures, it assumes a 'personal' dimension, for it consists of an active, conscious and loving will to save all creatures: to speak of such a will is to speak of some kind of 'person' directing that will.

In one respect, then, this can be seen as a personalization of the Absolute, bestowing upon the pure, ineffable Absolute a personal or anthropomorphic dimension, a dimension without which it cannot enter into engagement with human persons. For the pure Absolute has no relation whatsoever with any conceivable relativity. But this personal dimension does not in any way diminish the absoluteness of the Absolute. For the manifestation of such qualities as compassion, love, and mercy does not exhaust the nature of the Principle thus manifested. As stressed before, the Absolute is the Essence, transcending the Names and Qualities which are assumed by the Absolute in its relationship with the world; transcending these Names and Qualities implies transcending those 'personal' dimensions of God which, precisely, are designated by the Names and Qualities. In this way, the Islamic synthesis between two conceptions of God can be seen as analogous to the Mahayana-Hinayāna polarity within Buddhism. For the personal and supra-personal aspects of Allāh, comprising all the qualities designated by all of the divine Names, are in perfect harmony and perfect synchronicity. There is no contradiction between asserting on the one hand that the Essence of God infinitely transcends all conceivable 'personal' qualities, and on the other, that God assumes these personal qualities for the sake of entering into compassionate, enlightening and saving relationship with His creatures. This Islamic synthesis can help to show that what has been called Mahayana 'theism' in no way compromises early Buddhism's insistence on the transcendence of the *Dhamma/ Nirvana/Shūnya* vis-à-vis all conceivable qualities.

Oneness and Compassion

Islam also helps to answer the question which might be posed to a Buddhist: what is the connection between the metaphysics of unity— in terms of which there appears to be no 'other', no 'dualism', *Samsara* and *Nirvana* being one—and the quality of compassion—which logically presupposes both an agent and a recipient of compassion, thus, a duality? Or it might be asked: is there a contradiction between the absolute transcendence of Reality, and the compassionate manifestation of this Reality? We would answer in terms of Islamic metaphysics that the oneness of Reality strictly *implies* compassion. For the oneness of God is not simply exclusive, it is also inclusive—it is both *Ahad* and *Wāhid*, it is both transcendent and immanent. As *al-Wāhid*, all-inclusive oneness, God encompasses all things, whence such divine Names as *al-Wasi'*, 'the Infinitely Capacious' and *al-Muhīt*, 'the All-Encompassing'. Now it is from this all-embracing dimension of divine reality that compassion springs: for it is not just as being or knowledge, presence or immanence, that God encompasses all, it is also as *Rahma*: *My Rahma encompasses all things*, as we saw above. The angels, indeed, give priority to God's *Rahma* over His knowledge (*'Ilm*) when addressing Him as the one who encompasses all things: *You encompass all things in* Rahma *and* 'Ilm (40:7).[34]

It might still be objected: God is certainly 'merciful' but He should not be called 'compassionate' as He does not 'suffer' with any creature. Mercy, it will be argued, is the more appropriate word by which to translate *Rahma*. One may reply as follows: insofar as compassion is a human virtue, it cannot but be rooted in a divine quality; it is this divine quality of *Rahma* which serves as the transcendent archetype of the human virtue of compassion. The relationship between this divine quality and its human reflection is characterised by two apparently contradictory principles: similarity (*tashbīh*) and incomparability (*tanzīh*). Thus, in respect

---

34. It is interesting to note that in Tibetan Buddhism, there is likewise a certain priority of compassion over knowledge, as far as the manifestation of these qualities is concerned on earth, for the Dalai Lama, representing the Bodhisattva of compassion (Chenrezig, the Tibetan name of Avalokiteshvara) has priority over the Panchen Lama, who represents the Buddha of Light (Opagmed, the Tibetan name for Amitābha). See M. Pallis, *The Way and the Mountain* (London: Peter Owen, 1991), pp. 161–162.

of *tashbīh*, God as 'The Compassionate' can metaphorically be said to manifest sympathy for us in our suffering; and it is out of this 'com-passion or 'sym-pathy' that He graciously lifts us out of our suffering. However this conception needs its complement: the point of view deriving from the principle of *tanzīh*: inasmuch as the quality designated by 'The Compassionate' has no self-subsistent essence, but subsists solely through the Essence as such, it cannot possibly be subject to any relativity. The inner dimension of this divine quality must perforce transcend the sphere within which suffering and other such relativities are situated, failing which it would not be a *transcendent* quality, that is: one that is rooted in the utter transcendence of the divine Essence.

Conversely, on the human plane, compassion as *Rahma* is evidently a virtue which one must acquire and cultivate; it must therefore be present in God, failing which our human quality of compassion would lack any divine principle, compassion would then be a human effect without a divine cause. This is made clear in the prophetic saying on the *Rahma* of the mother for her child: human compassion is akin to the compassion of God for all creatures, except that divine compassion is absolute and infinite, while human compassion is relative and finite. The essence of the quality is one and the same, only its ontological intensity, or mode of manifestation, is subject to gradation.

The aspect of transcendence proper to God implies that this attribute, when ascribed to God, has an absolute and infinite quality, in contrast to the relative, finite participation in that quality by human beings. In the human context, then, compassion manifests two things: a virtue whose essence is divine, on the one hand, and a human capacity to suffer, on the other. In the divine context, the transcendent source of human compassion is affirmed, but the susceptibility to suffering which accompanies the human condition, is totally absent. As between the human virtue and the divine quality— or simply: between the human and the divine—there is both essential continuity and existential discontinuity, analogical participation and ontological distinction, *tashbīh* and *tanzīh*.

Another way of resolving the apparent contradiction between divine compassion and divine unity is provided by al-Ghazālī. If compassion be understood as a mode of love, then one can reformulate the question and ask whether it is possible to ascribe love to God: can God be susceptible to desire for His creatures, when

He possesses perfectly and infinitely all that He could possibly desire? Can the Absolute desire the relative? Al-Ghazālī addresses this question, first in theological mode, and then in terms of metaphysics of oneness, from the point of view of *ma'rifa*. One can legitimately apply the same word, love (*mahabba*), both to man and to God; but the meaning of the word changes depending on the agent of love. Human love is defined as an inclination (*mayl*) of the soul towards that which is in harmony with it, beauty both outward and inward, seeking from another soul the consummation of love. Through this love it attains completeness, a mode of perfection which cannot be attained within itself. Such love, al-Ghazālī asserts, cannot be ascribed to God, in whom all perfections are infinitely and absolutely realized. However, one can say that God loves His creatures, from a higher, metaphysical point of view. God's love is absolutely real, but His love is not for any 'other' being or entity. Rather, it is for Himself: for His own Essence, qualities and acts, this constituting the entirety of being. Hence, when the Qur'ān asserts that '*He loves them*' (5:54), this means that 'God does indeed love them [all human souls], but in reality He loves nothing other than Himself, in the sense that He is the totality [of being], and there is nothing in being apart from Him.'[35]

Al-Ghazālī demonstrates that God is the entirety of being by reference to the holy utterance cited earlier: 'My slave draws near to Me through nothing I love more than that which I have made obligatory for him. My slave never ceases to draw near to Me through supererogatory acts until I love him. And when I love him, I am his hearing by which he hears, his sight by which he sees, his hand by which he grasps, and his foot by which he walks.'

It is the saint, the *walī Allāh* (literally: friend of God), who comes to understand the reality that God alone is—that there is no reality but the divine reality—and this understanding comes through effacement, *fanā'*, in that reality, and this, in turn is the function of God's love: 'My slave never ceases to draw near ... until I *love* him.' It is from this divine love that the saint comes to see that God loves all creatures, and that the reality of this love is constituted by God's infinite love of Himself. This love is ex-

---

35. Al-Ghazālī is here citing the saying of Shaykh Sa'īd al-Mayhinī. This is from 'The Book of love and longing and intimacy and contentment' of his *Ihyā'*, book 6, part 4, vol. 5, p. 221.

pressed not just by the term *mahabba* but also by *Rahma*, which *encompasses all things*.

* * *

It may appear at first sight that such metaphysical and cosmic dimensions of compassion in Islam can only compared with similar dimensions within Mahayana Buddhism. The Theravada teachings on compassion seem to be more psychological and individual than cosmic and universal. For example, reading the following text, one might think that compassion is exhausted by one dimension only: the compassion inherent in the teaching of the *Dhamma*.

'I will teach you, brethren, the Uncompounded and the way going to the Uncompounded. Now what, brethren, is the Uncompounded? The destruction of lust, of hatred, of delusion, brethren, is called the Uncompounded. And what, brethren, is the way going to the Uncompounded? It is mindfulness relating to the sphere of the body that is so called. Thus, brethren, have I shown you the Uncompounded, and the way going to it. Whatever can be done by a teacher desirous of the welfare of his disciples, out of compassion for them, that have I done for you, brethren.' [36]

But this dimension should be seen only as the ultimate pedagogical form taken by compassion, and it does not exclude, still less deny, the cosmic and universal dimensions of compassion. For example, also in the Pali canon we find such passages as the following:

May all beings be at ease, secure;
May they all be happy in heart.
Whoever is a breathing being,
Stable or unstable without exception,
Long or those who are large,
Medium, short, subtle gross.
Visible or invisible, distant or near.
Beings or those yet to be born,
May they all be happy in heart. [37]

Here one observes that the moral quality of compassion is to be extended to all beings without exception, and surpasses pedagogi-

36. *Samyutta Nikāya*, 4:359. Cited in *Some Buddhist Sayings*, op. cit., p. 322.
37. *Khuddaka Pātha*, 8–9. Cited by Phra Soonthorndhammathada in *Compassion in Buddhism and Purānas* (Delhi: Nag Publishers, 1995), p. 94.

cal or psychological or individual modalities. Here, we find a resonance with Islam, for if God's *Rahma* encompasses all, if His grace is bestowed on both those who reject Him and accept Him, the Muslim likewise must reflect this divine quality and be compassionately predisposed to all beings: one must possess, in other words, a compassionate 'prejudice', which is one application of a principle of inter-personal relations very strongly emphasized in the corpus of prophetic sayings: one must always have, as an a priori disposition towards one's fellow beings, 'a good opinion' (*husn al-zann*), rather than its opposite, *sū' al-zann*, suspicion.

Likewise from the Pali canon, we find this expression of the all-encompassing nature of compassion: 'Making the whole world of beings the object of these minds endowed with compassion, we will continue to relate to the whole world with minds that are like the earth—untroubled, free from enmity, vast, enlarged and measureless (*appamāna*).'[38] Similarly, the Buddha taught his followers to cultivate compassion so that they come to resemble 'space which cannot be painted', or 'the Ganges which cannot be burned.'[39]

The Buddha defined 'liberation of the mind' quite simply as 'compassion' (*Anguttara Nikāya*, 1:4). It is interesting to read the traditional commentary on this, *Manorathapūrnī*:

> The liberation of the mind is love and compassion. It is compassion as it relates to all sentient beings with the wish for their welfare ... since the mind conjoined with compassion is liberated from all adverse factors such as the hindrances [*nivārana*: sense-desire, anger, agitation, laziness, doubt] and so forth, it is called a liberation of the mind.[40]

Here we see that compassion is not just expressed by the teacher enlightening his disciple; it is here seen to be a factor disposing one to enlightenment, thus, a subjective condition for engaging with the meditative means of enlightenment rather than only an objective transmission of those means of enlightenment. So, before being capable of eliminating one's own suffering through enlightenment, one has to feel compassion for the suffering of all others.

This universal compassion is referred to by the Buddha as the 'soil' within which concentration is to be cultivated. But it is also the

---

38. *Majjhima Nikāya*, 1:27. Cited in *Compassion in Buddhism*, op. cit., p. 93.
39. Ibid., p. 93.
40. Cited in *Compassion in Buddhism*, op. cit.,,pp. 83–84.

fruit of enlightenment, for even when full enlightenment is attained, this meditative compassion for all is permanently maintained as a feature of the mind of the enlightened one.[41]

Rahma as Creator

Turning now to another aspect of compassion, that of its creative power, we see again that what is left implicit in early Buddhism is rendered altogether explicit both in Islam and in such Mahayana traditions as Jodo Shin. In both traditions, the Creator is nothing other than the 'All-Compassionate', or the 'All-Loving'; but whereas this conception is enshrined in the very heart of the Qur'ān, it emerges in Buddhism only in certain Mahayana traditions.

As was noted above, the Muslim consecrates every important action with the utterance of the *basmala*, the phrase: *Bismillāh al-Rahmān al-Rahīm*, in the Name of God, the Lovingly Compassionate, the Lovingly Merciful. This formula also initiates each of the 114 chapters of the Qur'ān (except one). It is altogether appropriate that all ritual and significant action be initiated with a recollection of the compassionate source of creation. In terms of the two divine Names deriving from the root of *Rahma*, the first, *al-Rahmān* is normally used to refer to the creative power of *Rahma*, and the second, *al-Rahīm*, to its salvific power. Combining these two properties of loving compassion, the creative and redemptive, one sees that ultimately nothing can escape or be separated from God's all-embracing *Rahma*. This is why calling upon *al-Rahmān* is tantamount to calling upon God: *Call upon Allāh or call upon al-Rahmān* (17:110). If *al-Rahmān* is so completely identified with the very substance of God, then it follows that the *Rahma* which so quintessentially defines the divine nature is not simply 'mercy' or 'compassion' but is rather the infinite love and perfect beatitude of ultimate reality, which overflows into creation in the myriad forms assumed by mercy and compassion, peace and love.

Rahma is thus to be understood primarily in terms of a love which gives of itself: what it gives is what it is, transcendent beatitude, which creates out of love, and, upon contact with Its creation, assumes the nature of loving compassion and mercy, these being the dominant motifs of the relationship between God and the world. As was seen above, God's transcendent *Rahma* is alluded to by the Prophet in terms of the most striking expression of *Rahma* on

---

41. *Anguttara Nikāya*, 1:181–184, cited in ibid., p. 97.

earth—that expressed by a mother who, after searching frantically for her baby, clutches it to her breast and feeds it.

As was cited above: *Call upon Allāh or call upon al-Rahmān; whichever you call upon, unto Him belong the most beautiful names* (17:110). It should be noted in this verse that all the names are described as 'most beautiful', including therefore all the names of rigour as well as those of gentleness. But the most important point to note here is that the name *al-Rahmān* is practically co-terminous with the name *Allāh*, indicating that the quality of loving mercy takes us to the very heart of the divine nature. In two verses we are told that *Rahma* is 'written' upon the very Self of God: *He has written mercy upon Himself* (6:12); *Your Lord has written mercy upon Himself* (6:54). The word *kataba*, 'he wrote', implies a kind of inner prescription, so that *Rahma* can be understood as a kind of inner law governing the very *nafs*, the Self or Essence of God. The use of the image of 'writing' here can be seen as a metaphor for expressing the metaphysical truth that *Rahma* is as it were 'inscribed' within the deepest reality of the divine nature. God's 'inscription' *upon* Himself is thus God's description *of* Himself, of His own deepest nature.

The creative aspect of the divine *Rahma* is vividly brought home in the chapter entitled '*al-Rahmān*' (Sūra 55); it is *al-Rahmān* who *taught the Qur'ān, created man, taught him discernment* (verses 2–4). The whole of this chapter evokes and invokes the reality of this quintessential quality of God. The blessings of Paradise are described here in the most majestic and attractive terms; but so too are the glories, beauties and harmonies of God's entire cosmos, including all the wonders of virgin nature, these verses being musically punctuated by the refrain: *so which of the favours of your Lord can you deny?* In this chapter named after *al-Rahmān*, then, we are invited to contemplate the various levels at which *Rahma* fashions the substance of reality: the *Rahma* that describes the deepest nature of the divine; the *Rahma* that is musically inscribed into the very recitation of the chapter; the *Rahma* that creates all things; the *Rahma* that reveals itself through the Qur'ān and through all the signs (*āyāt*) of nature. One comes to see that God has created not only *by Rahma*, and *from Rahma* but also *for Rahma*: … *except those upon whom God has mercy: for this did He create them* (11:119); and *within Rahma*: *My Rahma encompasses all things* (7:156).

Combining these two properties of loving compassion, the creative and redemptive, or the ontological and salvific, we see why it is that ultimately nothing can escape or be separated from God's all-embracing *Rahma*, which is the divine matrix containing the cosmos. The word 'matrix' should be taken quite literally, in relation to its root: 'mother'. The word for womb, *rahim*, derives from the same root as *Rahma*. The entire cosmos is not just brought into being by *Rahma*, it is perpetually encompassed by *Rahma* which nourishes it at every instant, as the mother's womb nourishes and encompasses the embryo growing within it. As we saw above, the *Tathāgatagarbha*, literally means: the 'womb' of the Tathāgata, the 'one thus gone'. This womb or matrix not only contains all things, it is also contained within the soul, being one with the immanent Buddha-nature (*Buddhadhatu*) which each individual must strive to realize.

The analogy evoked by this etymological relationship between maternal love and the compassionate matrix of creation is mysteriously implied in the chapter of the Qur'ān named after the Blessed Virgin, the *Sūrat Maryam* (chapter 19). For in this chapter we notice that the name *al-Rahmān* is mentioned repeatedly as a virtual synonym for God: the Blessed Virgin seeks refuge in *al-Rahmān* (19:18), she consecrates her fast to *al-Rahmān* (19:26), Satan is described as the enemy of *al-Rahmān* (19:44), when the verses revealed by *al-Rahmān* are recited, the Prophets fall down prostrate (19:58), and so on. The name *al-Rahmān* is repeated no less than 16 times—more times than in any other chapter of the Qur'ān. Since this name occurs altogether 57 times in the *sūras* of the Qur'ān (apart from its occurrence at the head of every chapter but one), this means that the *Sūrat Maryam* contains more than one quarter of all the instances in which the name *al-Rahmān* comes in the Qur'ān.[42]

These considerations help to substantiate the point made above: that in the Islamic worldview, God's *Rahma* is not just mercy; rather it is the infinite love and overflowing beatitude of ultimate reality, one of whose manifestations is mercy. In this light, one can better appreciate such perspectives as the following, within Jodo Shin Buddhism:

> The inner truth is: 'From the Eternal Love do all beings have their birth'.[43]

---

42. The name *al-Rahīm* occurs 95 times, apart from its occurrence in the *basmala*. The root, *r-h-m* and its derivatives occurs 375 times, not including the 114 instances of the *basmala*.

43. Kenryo Kanamatsu, *Naturalness—A Classic of Shin Buddhism,* op. cit., p. 113.

Such a statement articulates a dimension of causality left completely out of account by the earlier Buddhist scriptures, where the entire emphasis was on escape from the round of births and deaths. The only important point about the 'birth' of beings was the existence of the 'unborn' to which one must flee for refuge: the process by which beings were born was thus seen as a process of enslavement to the ineluctability of suffering and death. In Mahayana Buddhism, however, one can find expressions of love and compassion which are identified with the creative power of the Absolute. This passage from *Naturalness* shows that the Absolute reveals its 'Eternal Life' through the dimension of its 'Great Compassion':

> Amida is the Supreme Spirit from whom all spiritual revelations grow, and to whom all personalities are related. Amida is at once the Infinite Light (*Amitābha*) and the Eternal Life (*Amitāyus*). He is at once the Great Wisdom (*Mahāprajna: daichi*)—the Infinite Light—and the Great Compassion (*Mahākaruna: daihi*)—the Eternal Life. The Great Compassion is creator while the Great Wisdom contemplates.[44]

Some lines later, we read about the unitive power of love; this can be compared with the compassionate love which is spiritually required and logically implied by the metaphysics of *tawhīd*: 'In love ... the sense of difference is obliterated and the human heart fulfils its inherent purpose in perfection, transcending the limits of itself and reaching across the threshold of the spirit-world.'[45]

In love, *the sense of difference is obliterated*: the unity of being, which may be conceptually *understood* through knowledge, is spiritually *realized* through love, whose infinite creativity overflows into a compassion whose most merciful act is to reveal this very oneness. To return to al-Ghazālī: the perfect and eternal love of God creates the human being in a disposition which ever seeks proximity to Him, and furnishes him with access to the pathways leading to the removal of the veils separating him from God, such that he comes to 'see' God by means of God Himself. 'And all this is the act of God, and a grace bestowed upon him [God's creature]: and such is what is meant by God's love of him.'[46] This enlightening grace of God towards His creatures is constitutive of His love for them, a love

---

44. Ibid., p. 63.
45. Ibid., p. 64.
46. Al-Ghazālī, *Ihyā'*, op. cit., pp. 221–222.

which in reality is nothing other than His love for Himself. Human love and compassion, by means of which *the sense of difference is obliterated* between self and other, can thus be seen as a unitive reflection herebelow of the oneness of the love of God for Himself within Himself. Absolute compassion and transcendent oneness, far from being mutually exclusive are thus harmoniously integrated in an uncompromisingly unitive *tawhīd*.

The compassion which we have been examining is clearly an overflow of the beatitude which defines an essential aspect of ultimate Reality, the oneness of which embraces all things by virtue of this compassion, precisely. Inward beatitude, proper to the One, and outward compassion, integrating the many, is a subtle and important expression of the spiritual mystery of *tawhīd*. We observe in this affirmation of *tawhīd* another conceptual resonance between the two traditions, a resonance made clear by the following verses of Milarepa:

> Without realizing the truth of Many-Being-One
> Even though you meditate on the Great Light,
> You practice but the View-of-Clinging.
> Without realizing the unity of Bliss and Void,
> Even though on the Void you meditate,
> You practice only nihilism.[47]

The truth of 'Many-Being-One' can be read as a spiritual expression of *tawhīd*, and mirrors many such expressions in Islamic mysticism, indeed, the literal meaning of *tawhīd* being precisely a dynamic integration, not just a static oneness. It is derived from the form of the verb, *wahhada*, meaning 'to make one'. Phenomenal diversity is thus integrated into principial unity by means of the vision unfolding from this understanding of *tawhīd*. In these verses, Milarepa tells one of his disciples that however much he may meditate on the supernal Light, if he regards that Light as being separate from all things by way of transcendence, then he cannot realize the immanence of that Light in all that exists, that immanence by virtue of which the 'many' become 'one', the 'face' of reality being visible in everything that exists. In the absence of this vision, then meditation on the Light results only in 'clinging'—clinging, that is, to a false distinction between the One and the many, a duality which will imprison the meditator within the realm of multiplicity. It is

---

47. *The Hundred Thousand Songs of Milarepa*, op. cit., vol. 2, p. 526.

when Milarepa addresses the intrinsic nature of the Void, however, that the similarity with the Islamic conception of the beatific *rahma* of God emerges in a striking manner. 'Without realizing the unity of Bliss and Void', any meditation on the Void is but nihilistic. The Void is intrinsically blissful, or it is not the Void. We saw earlier that *Nirvana* and the Void (*Shūnya*) are essentially one, the term *Nirvana* stressing the blissful nature of the state wherein one is conscious of the Absolute, and the term 'Void' stressing the objective nature of the Absolute, transcending all things are 'full'—of false being. Milarepa's verse makes clear this identity of essence, and shows moreover that it is precisely because the Void is overflowing with beatitude that the experience of the Void cannot but be blissful: it is far from a nihilistic negation of existence and thought. Knowing and experiencing the beatitude of the Void thus cannot but engender in the soul a state of being reflecting this beatitude, and a wish to share that beatitude with all beings: such a wish being the very essence of compassion, which is not simply a capacity to feel the suffering of others as one's own—which articulates one level of ethical *tawhīd*—but also, at a higher level of *tawhīd*, a capacity to bring that suffering to an end through making accessible the mercy and felicity ever-flowing from ultimate Reality. This is the message—which is immediately intelligible to any Muslim—of the following verses of Milarepa:

> If in meditation you still tend to strive,
> Try to arouse for all a great compassion,
> Be identified with the All-Merciful.[48]

Here, we see the All-Merciful being identified with Absolute Reality, referred to earlier as the Void, but here, the character of the Void is clearly affirmed as infinite mercy. To identify with this mercy is to identify with the Absolute; arousing for all 'a great compassion' means infusing into one's soul a quality which reflects the infinite compassion of the Absolute. One from whom compassion flows to all is one in whom 'the overflowing Void-Compassion', as Milarepa calls it in another verse, has been realized: it ceaselessly overflows from the Absolute to the relative, and to the extent that one has made oneself 'void' for its sake, one becomes a vehicle for the transmission of the Compassion of the Void:

---

48. Ibid., vol. 2, p. 561.

Rechungpa, listen to me for a moment.
From the centre of my heart stream
Glowing beams of light.
…
This shows the unity of mercy and the Void.[49]

* * *

To conclude this section, it may be objected that however remarkable be the similarities between the Islamic and the Jodo Shin conceptions of the loving compassion that articulates the creativity of the Absolute, Jodo Shin cannot be taken as representative of the broad Buddhist tradition, and is rather an exception proving the rule. To this, we would reply that the Jodo Shin presentation of this crucial theme—God as Creator through compassion—does not prove that the two traditions of Islam and Buddhism can be crudely equated as regards this theme; rather, it simply demonstrates that the differences between the Islamic conception of God as Creator through compassion and the Buddhist silence on the question of such a Creator need not be seen as the basis for a reciprocal rejection. Rather, the very fact that at least one Buddhist school of thought affirms the idea of a compassionate Creator shows that there is no absolute incompatibility between the two traditions as regards this principle. There is no need to claim that the principle plays an analogous role in both traditions, far from it: definitive, central and inalienable in Islam; and conceivable, possible, and, at least, not absolutely undeniable in Buddhism.

---

49. Ibid., vol. 2, p. 445.

Epilogue
The Common Ground of Sanctity

The following passage from the *Prajnopāyaviniscayasiddhi*, an important text in the Mahayana tradition, expresses that dazzling combination of wisdom and compassion, knowledge of the One and compassion for all beings, which constitutes the essence of sanctity.

The non-substantiality of things which is realized by reflection and by discriminating between the act of knowing and what is known, is called the essence of Wisdom. Because one is passionately devoted to all beings who have failed to extricate themselves from a whole flood of suffering, this passionate devotion, of which their suffering is the cause, is known as Compassion. In that, one thereby brings a man to the desired end by a combination of appropriate measures; it is also called the Means (*upāya*).

The mingling of both [wisdom and compassion] is known as Wisdom-Means in a union free of duality. It is the essence of Dharma, to which nothing may be added and from which nothing may be withdrawn. It is free from the two notions of subject and object, free from being and non-being, from characterizing and characteristics; it is pure and immaculate in its own nature. Neither duality nor non-duality, calm and tranquil, it consists in all things, motionless and unflurried; such is Wisdom-Means, which may be known intuitively. It is this that is called the supreme and wondrous abode of all Buddhas, the Dharma-sphere, the divine cause of the perfection of bliss. It is Nirvana Indeterminate (*apratisthitanirvāna*) … it is the blissful stage of self-consecration (*svadhithāna*), the beatitude of the perfection of Wisdom. The three Buddha-bodies, the three Buddhist vehicles, mantras in their innumerable thousands … phenomenal existence and that which transcends it, arise from the same source … It is called the Great Bliss … the Supreme One, the Universal Good, the producer of Perfect Enlightenment. The great sages define this truth, which is the supreme bliss of self and others, as the union of limitless Compassion—which is intent alone on the destruction of the world's suffering—and of perfect Wisdom, which is free from all attachment, and is an accumulation of knowledge which may not be reckoned, so great is its diversity'.[1]

The perfect realization of oneness, together with its concomitants of wisdom and compassion, is expressed in the very definition of sanctity or *walāya*, cited above:

> My slave draws near to Me through nothing I love more than that which I have made obligatory for him. My slave never ceases to draw near to Me through supererogatory acts until I love him. And when I love him, I am his hearing by which he hears, his sight by which he sees, his hand by which he grasps, and his foot by which he walks.

God's love is at one with His compassion, which in turn is 'written' upon His very Self; when God so loves His slave that He hears, sees and acts through him, then the substance of all that comes from such a being can only be divine love in union with perfect knowledge. It is this combination of wisdom and love at the highest and deepest levels which arises out of the realization of *tawhīd*, which is not just affirming one, but 'realizing one', making real the One both transcendent and immanent. This transmission of divine reality through the saint implies no compromise as regards the principle of divine transcendence. On the contrary, the saint provides the most dramatic and irrefutable evidence of the most radical *tawhīd*; only the saint can do this, for he alone is truly effaced before God, and it is by virtue of this effacement that the divine Face manifests through him: the spotless mirror of the saint's heart faithfully reflects the Face of God whose infinite transcendence is rendered no less transcendent by virtue of this dazzling reflection on earth. This perfect reflection of the divine Face transmits the essential quality of the divine nature, not just the love by virtue of which the saint comes to hear and see and act through God, but also loving compassion, that *Rahma* which is inscribed in the very Self of God. The saint thus comes to participate in the process by which divine compassion and the divine knowledge embrace all things: *You encompass all things in loving compassion and knowledge* (40:7). Divine knowledge or wisdom is thus inseparable from divine compassion: to plumb the essence of the one is to

---

1. *Prajnopāyaviniscayasiddhi*, ch. 1–3; cited in *Buddhist Texts*, op. cit., pp. 241–242.

enter into the essence of the other. When the Prophet is described as a *rahma* for the whole of creation (21:107), this implies that he is likewise a source of wisdom for the whole of creation. The saint is able, in the measure of his effacement before the Face of God, to participate in this holy embrace of the whole of creation by the qualities, at once prophetic and divine, of wisdom and compassion.

* * *

The common ground upon which the spiritual traditions of Islam and Buddhism stand together is the principle of absolute oneness, that to which the revealed texts of both traditions bear witness, and the realization of which, by the individual soul, here and now, constitutes the ultimate goal of both religions. It is in relation to the concomitants of oneness that holiness or sanctity is defined in both religions: oneness demands perfect knowledge, which in turn requires the total effacement of oneself within that knowledge, and the unconditional gift of oneself to others in compassion. The saint—the *walī* in Islam and the Arahat/Bodhisattva in Buddhism—represents the summit of human perfection; it is in the saint that the deepest aims of religion are consummated in the world; it is by the saint that the religion is realized in all its plenitude; it is through the saint that the holiness of the religion is most palpably experienced. Theory and practice, concept and realization, spiritual ideals and human realities—all are united in the person of the saint. The two basic dimensions of holiness—vertical and horizontal, metaphysical and ethical, divine and human—can be seen to define the essential common ground bringing together Islam and Buddhism in a common aspiration for the One.

Buddha in the Qur'ān?
by Shaykh Hamza Yusuf

When Buddhism and Islam are considered together, some see it as a matter of comparing apples and oranges. Upon deeper examination, there is—like the two savory grown-on-trees, seeds-in-the-flesh fruit—much which the two faiths have in common. Buddhism sees itself as a reformist movement that emerged from the preceding Hindu tradition. Similarly, Islam sees itself as a reformist movement, one that emerged from the preceding Abrahamic traditions and in response to perceived Jewish and Christian spiritual dissipation. Both Buddhism and Islam have universalist claims, with strong core doctrines, such as the five pillars and six articles of faith in Islam, and the four noble truths and the noble eightfold path in Buddhism. But perhaps most significant is that both are rooted in deeply rich ethical canons that consider kindness, compassion, and mercy as the core human qualities to be nurtured. In his talks throughout the world, the Dalai Lama emphasizes similar virtues, and the Qur'ān calls the Prophet Muhammad ﷺ "a mercy to all the worlds" (21:107).

While many similarities can be discerned, there is also a shared history that has been mutually beneficial for both traditions, especially for the Muslims, because it prompted them to discuss how to deal—theologically and legally—with religions they had newly encountered. When the early Muslim dynasties conquered lands in Iran, Afghanistan, and Central Asia, not to mention the Indian subcontinent, they found large Buddhist populations, and they looked to the Qur'ān and the Sunnah[1] for guidance.

The Qur'ān discusses categories of belief in the surah[2] entitled, "The Pilgrimage," which is one of the most important surahs dealing with other faiths and beliefs, and it contains several verses that

---

1. The Sunnah is the normative practice of the Prophet Muhammad ﷺ. For example, it was the Sunnah of the Prophet ﷺ to take an afternoon nap. The Arabic word *sunnah* is derived from a root meaning "way, practice." The Prophet ﷺ said, "I have left for you two things: the Qur'ān and my Sunnah; if you cling to them, you will not go astray" (narrated by Imam Mālik in *al-Muwattā'*). The Sunnah is derived from the words, actions, and tacit approvals and disapprovals of the Prophet ﷺ. It is the second most important source of authority and legislation in Islam after the Qur'ān.

2. Surah refers to a chapter in the Qur'ān. The Arabic word *sūrah* is derived from a root meaning "wall, form," as each surah's function is to wall in and provide form to one section of the Qur'ān.

directly address religious diversity.[3] The most definitive verse of this surah in this regard distinguishes between six categories of religious belief, and Muslim exegetes have traditionally placed all religions and sects into one of these six: "As for the Muslims, the Jews, the Sabians, the Christians, the Magians, and the polytheists, God will decide among them on the day of resurrection" (22:17). The weighty import of this verse is that it is theologically prohibited for us to condemn any individual, irrespective of his or her faith, to damnation or punishment in the afterlife because ultimate judgment belongs to God alone. Many hadith[4] and statements of the companions of the Prophet ﷺ also affirm this fundamental article of faith.

So where did Muslims traditionally place the Buddhists among these six categories? Unlike many modern Muslims who consider Buddhists to be among the polytheists, believing them to be idolators due to the profusion of images and statues of the Buddha, early Muslim scholars of comparative religion had a very different view. They held a favorable opinion of Buddhists and marveled at the profound spirituality of Buddhist practitioners.

In classical Muslim literature on religions and sects, we find many references to "al-Badadah," meaning the Buddhists, as well as to "al-Budd," the Buddha himself. Ibn al-Nadīm (d. 998), an Iraqi bookseller and author of the famous work entitled *The Compendium* (*al-Fihrist*), who catalogued existing authors and their subjects of study, records books that deal with Buddhism, including *The Life of Buddha* (*Kitāb al-Budd*). In his chapter entitled "Notes on the Buddha," Ibn al-Nadīm delineates the different scholarly views of the Buddha: some believed he was the divine incarnate,[5] while others

---

3. See the section entitled "Qur'ānic premises of dialogue," pp. 12-14 in Reza Shah-Kazemi's text for further discussion of this theme.

4. The hadith are statements attributed to the Prophet Muhammad ﷺ by which his Sunnah is known. They constitute the sayings of the Prophet ﷺ as well as the sayings of his companions that narrate his actions or descriptions. The hadith are considered an authoritative source of legislation and constitute a major source of guidance for Muslims, second only to the Qur'ān. They were originally orally transmitted and passed down using a rigorous method of authentication and were compiled from the beginning of the latter part of the first century of the Islamic era into the fourth century.

5. While there are some Buddhists who see the Buddha as a divine being, which for Muslims would constitute clear idolatry (*shirk*), many Buddhists do not. Mu Soeng comments, "For the Sthaviras, the Buddha Shakyamuni was a historical personage—a great teacher but not a divinity." While Mahayana expressions of devotion can be construed as idolatrous, Theravada Buddhism is less so, but Bud-

claimed he was a messenger of God; still others thought Buddha to be a generic name for those who guided others onto the right path. He describes the extraordinary images of the Buddha in Bamiyan, (in what is today called Afghanistan), and writes that statues of the Buddha were brought from there to Baghdad. He also mentions the Nava Vihara monastery, the famous site of pilgrimage in the same region that was visited by Buddhists from far and wide, by land and by sea. He writes of the Golden Temple that he learned of from an Indian source he trusted, who said that pilgrims seeking cures found that upon seeing the temple, God healed their ailments.[6]

Perhaps the most significant classical Muslim description of Buddhism is found in Imam Muhammad b. 'Abd al-Karīm al-Shahrastānī's (d. 1153) comprehensive survey entitled, *Religions and Sects* (*al-Milal wa al-nihal*). Imam al-Shahrastānī was a notable Shafi'ī jurist, Ash'arī theologian, and author of the most celebrated and cited work on comparative religion in the pre-modern Islamic tradition.[7]

In this work, he also makes a rather stunning—and intriguing—statement connecting the Buddha to a character in the Qur'ān.

***

Before we explore that assertion, it is worth noting that Imam al-Shahrastānī identifies the Buddhists as Sabians, which is a consequential categorization, given the status that Sabians have in the Qur'ān as a saved group. The root word of Sabians is *saba'*, which is "the rising of a star." Most exegetes explain that the Sabians worshipped the stars because they believed the stars are vehicles by which God organizes the world. In several commentaries, the Sabians are also described as believing in reincarnation and the eternity

---

dhist priests have historically tolerated devotional expressions that often had their roots in previous idolatrous traditions of the peoples they encountered. Cha'n Buddhism rejects all forms of idolatry openly and in practice. See for further discussion Shah-Kazemi's text, section entitled "The Buddha as Messenger," pp. 14-19, and "Images of the Buddha, Blessings upon the Prophet," pp. 73-78.

6. Ibn Nadīm, *al-Fihrist*, (Beirut: Dār al-Ma'rifah, n.d), 486-489.

7. Imam Abū al-Fath Muhammad b. 'Abd al-Karīm al-Shahrastānī was a student of the erudite polymath theologian, Imam al-Qushayrī. He was born in Shahristan, an area between Nishapur and Khawarizm, and both these areas had large Buddhist populations. He became a popular preacher in Baghdad, and Ibn Khalikkān says about him, "He was an accomplished imam, jurist, and theologian, as well as a noted preacher. He is most famous for his book, *al-Milal wa al-nihal*, which attempts to give an account of all of the religions and sects known at that time."

of the world. They are sometimes erroneously identified with the Mandaean Sabians of Lower Iraq who held some Zoroastrian beliefs regarding light and darkness.

Shaykh Ibn Taymiyyah (d. 1255) believed that the Sabians were of two types: polytheistic and unitarian. According to him, they were people who did not have a law taken from a prophet, but he argues that there are also people among Jews, Christians, and Magians who, despite not having a religion *per se*, know God as one and do not deny God. He said they cling to a shared type of submission (*islām mushtarak*) that entails "worshipping God only, being truthful and just, prohibiting indecent and foul things, and prohibiting oppression as well as those other matters prophets were in agreement on." Furthermore, he affirms, "[They say,] 'There is no deity but God' despite having neither a revealed book nor a prophet."[8] He argues that the latter group refers to the Sabians included in the Qur'anic category of those who attain salvation. This is strengthened by the fact that the verse states that they believe in God and the Last Day. Furthermore, even if their beliefs are considered erroneous, this does not negate the possibility of their being saved on that day, according to the dominant theological position of the Ash'arī schools, since idolaters who were not recipients of a revealed message are not held accountable for not knowing—and accepting—divine unity.

In addition, hadith literature clearly indicates that some people with false beliefs will be saved in the afterlife. For example, according to a sound hadith, a man had his sons cremate him, hoping that God would not be able to recreate him and then punish him in the afterlife. The Prophet 🕮 informs us that God forgave the man, even though he doubted God's omnipotence, which is considered disbelief (*kufr*).[9] The verse in the Qur'ān categorizing those who will be saved states, "Surely those who believe, and the Jews, Christians, and Sabians, whoever believes in God and the Last Day, has their reward with their Lord and shall neither fear nor grieve" (2:62). Regarding this verse, Imam al-Alūsī (d. 1854), in his authoritative commentary, states:

> The Sabians are a group whose different schools revolved around a fanatical adherence to spiritual teachers

8. *Al-Mawsū'ah al-muyyassarah*, vol. 2, (Riyad, S.A., n.d.), 764.

9. For a more extensive examination of this problem, see my article, "Who are the Disbelievers?" *Seasons Journal*, vol. 5, no. 1, (San Francisco: Zaytuna Institute, 2008), 31-50.

(*ruhāniyyīn*) and taking intercessors. When they were unable to draw near through them directly and to take from their essences, some of them resorted to using pagodas.[10] So the Sabians of Asia Minor relied upon planets, and the Sabians of India relied upon stars, and some of them abandoned the temples and used images that can neither hear nor see or benefit anyone one iota. The first group consists of worshippers of planets and the second of idolaters. And each of the two groups [of Sabians] has many types and differs in their beliefs and rites. Imam Abū Hanīfah (d. 767) argues that they do not worship idols, but rather they exalt the stars, as the Kaaba, for example, is exalted [among Muslims].[11]

The Imam acknowledges here that Sabians are of different types and that among them are those in India as well as other places whose belief in the planets is clearly negated in Islam. It is impossible to know with any certainty whether the Buddhists as well as the Hindus can be included in this category, and scholars do not seem to have ever claimed this. But given the ambiguous language referring to Sabians and Magians that is used in the surahs al-Baqarah, al-Mā'idah, and al-Hajj, Muslims are advised to say "God knows best" (*Allāhu 'alam*).

The Abrahamic faiths' belief in God and the Last Day is not understood in the same manner in either Buddhism or Hinduism but certainly has parallels in both their teachings, especially in Pure Land Buddhism and philosophical Hinduism, which acknowledges one God and recognizes that the images in the temples are only aids to help simple people grasp a particular aspect of the universal, transcendent nature of God. While idolatry is an unpardonable sin in Islam, it is clear from the first prohibition the Qur'ān mentions, "And do not set up rivals with God, *knowingly*" (2:22), that it is predicated upon wittingly worshiping anything beside God or giving it attributes of divinity. Ignorance, according to the dominant opinion among Muslim scholars, is excused if no clear message—of

---

10. The word in the original Arabic text is *hayākil*, which can be glossed as a "temple or large alter." Al-Isfahānī says that it is "any large structure; a temple that Christians use that contains an image of Mary." Hence, it is a temple with an image, which is essentially what a pagoda is, and Webster's dictionary defines pagoda as "a religious building of the Far East," which is exactly what Imam al-Alūsī is referring to here. And God knows best.

11. See Imam al-Alūsī, *Ruh al-ma'ānī*, (2:62).

submission to God—has been given to a people. Imam al-Ghazzālī (d. 1111) argues that this exception also applies to those who receive a distorted presentation of Islam and reject it.[12]

***

In addition to including Buddhists among the Sabians, Imam al-Shahrastānī makes another remarkable assertion in *Religions and Sects* about the identity of the Buddha and a Qur'anic character. In a section entitled, "The Buddhists," he states:

> [The Buddhists believe] Buddha is a person from this world who is born and does not marry, eat, drink, age, or die. The first Buddha to manifest in the world is known as Shakyamuni, which means "honorable and noble." Between his appearance and the Hijrah is approximately 5000 years.[13] The next category below this is the Boddhisatva, which means "a seeker of the truth." One achieves this rank through patience and giving; and by desiring what should be desired; leaving attachment to this world; abandoning its appetites and pleasures; rising above its prohibited things; having mercy for all of creation; avoiding the ten sins: murder, theft, fornication, lying, dissention, foulness, cursing, name-calling, harshness, and denying the spiritual masters of the next life; and perfecting the ten virtues: generosity and charity, forgiving those who wrong you, overcoming anger with forbearance, relinquishing the pleasures of this world, meditating upon the eternal world and letting go of this ephemeral abode, exercising the intellect through study, comportment, and reflection upon the ends of matters, mastery of self-discipline by seeking the exalted, gentleness in word and deed toward everyone, conviviality with one's fraternity and preferring others to oneself, and complete detachment from creation with total inner disposition toward the Truth,

---

12. See Abū Hāmid al-Ghazzālī, *Majmū'at rasā'il al-Ghazzālī* (Beirut: Dār al-Kutub al-'Ilmiyyah, 1994), 96.

13. The author is off by about four thousand years. While al-Shahrastānī's account of Buddhism is somewhat flawed, it is remarkable for his time, and whatever errors it contains are no doubt a result of misinformation provided to him from his sources. While there is considerable debate on the exact date of the Buddha's birth, it is generally given around 563 BCE in Nepal. His death date was around 480 BCE, which would mean he preceded the Prophet 🕊 by approximately a thousand years, with about a 50-year margin of error.

extending one's entirety in rapturous desire of the Truth, in order to arrive at the gardens of Truth.... Among their scholars, they do not differ as to the eternity of the cosmos and their belief in *karma*, as previously mentioned. They emerged in India due to the special qualities of that land and its topography as well as the fact that among its peoples are those who excel in spiritual exercises and self-mastery. Based upon their description of the Buddha, if they are accurate, it would seem that he is none other than al-Khadir, whom Muslims acknowledge, upon him be peace.[14]

This last suggestion that there is a relationship between al-Khadir ﷺ and Buddha is noteworthy, and the commonalities between the two are worth contemplating. Although al-Khadir ﷺ is associated with the period of Moses ﷺ in the Qur'ān, a widespread belief among Muslims is that al-Khadir ﷺ does not die until the end of time. Hence, al-Shahrastānī would not have been troubled by this historical discrepancy--between the recorded historical dates of Moses ﷺ and the Buddha is a distance of approximately 700 years--since he would have most likely held the belief that al-Khadir ﷺ was a transhistorical character. It is also possible to interpret the figure of al-Khadir ﷺ as a supra-historical archetype, or a particular mode of spiritual guidance—antinomian and enigmatic, radically transcending human modes of comprehension, and even "normal" modes of prophetic guidance. Thus, rather than simply seeking to establish a historical connection or identification between al-Khadir ﷺ and the Buddha, one might also see the Buddha as *one* manifestation of the spiritual archetype articulated by the Qur'anic figure al-Khadir ﷺ. This point of view is substantiated by the remarkable parallels one sees between the two figures.

Al-Khadir ﷺ is indeed an enigmatic character. According to the Qur'ān, he is given two gifts directly from God: mercy and experiential knowledge of reality. He is generally not considered a prophet. He is a teacher who wants no students, and, in the Qur'anic narrative, he attempts to dissuade Moses ﷺ from attempting to learn what cannot be taught but has to be experienced. This is a very Bud-

---

14. Muhammad b. 'Abd al-Karīm al-Shahrastānī, *Kitāb al-milal wa al-nihal* (Beirut: Dār Kutub al-'Ilmiyyah, n.d.), 710-712. Given al-Shahrastānī's stature and status as an authoritative imam and his knowledge of Buddhism and Islamic theology, it is singularly noteworthy that he should suggest the possibility of the Buddha being the Qur'anic sage, al-Khadir ﷺ.

dhist view. The Buddha is reported to have said, "If one would make oneself as one teaches others to be, one should master self-control, for the self is truly hard to tame."[15] Al-Khadir ﷺ uses a Zen like approach, in which the student cannot discern the meaning of his actions but has to endure the teacher's outward antinomian behavior patiently. He is described by most of the theologians of Islam as someone who was given direct knowledge *('ilm ladunniyy)*, which is not revelation, but knowledge "from the divine presence." It is defined as:

> A direct knowledge someone obtains from God without means of an angel or a prophet through witnessing, as occurred with al-Khadir.... It is said that it is a knowledge of the divine essence and its qualities with a certainty that arises from direct witnessing and experience that occurs in the inner eye of consciousness.[16]

Sufi exegetes of the Qur'ān have argued:

> Al-Khidr represents the inner dimension, esoterism, which transcends form. He appears to men in those moments when their own soul bears witness to an awareness of that dimension. In that rare case when there is a spontaneous realization of spiritual truth on the part of a *fard*, a "solitary" or someone who is by destiny cut off from revelation or from normal channels of spiritual instruction, it is al-Khidr who is the teacher, as in the saying "when the disciple is ready, the master appears."[17]

The Sufi sage and recognized master Ibrāhīm b. Adham, who was a ruler of Balkh and abandoned his throne for a life of asceticism in the wilderness after al-Khadir ﷺ appeared to him twice, said, "In that wilderness I lived for four years. God gave me my eating without any toil of mine. Khidr the Green Ancient was my companion during that time—he taught me the Great Name of God."[18]

---

15. Thomas Cleary, *Dhammapada: The Sayings of Buddha* (New York: Bantam Books, 1994), 54.

16. See Dr. Anwar Fu'ād Abī Khuzām, *Mustalahāt al-Sūfiyyah* (Beirut: Maktabat Lubnan, 1993), 128.

17. Cyril Glasse, *The New Encyclopedia of Islam* (Walnut Creek, CA: AltaMira Press, 2003), 258. "Al-Khidr" is a variant spelling of "al-Khadir."

18. Ibid. Al-Khadir ﷺ is believed to be alive, and many Muslim saints throughout Islamic history have claimed to have met him and learned from him. There

According to a sound hadith related by Imam al-Bukhārī, the Prophet ﷺ stated that al-Khadir ﷻ was named so "because he sat upon white herbage under which green foliage sprouted forth."[19] This is an astonishing hadith, given that the Buddha is often depicted as sitting or walking upon large white lotus flowers with green foliage under them. The large white lotus flower also matches the Arabic description of *farwah bay\ā'*, a white "sheepskin-like plant"; given the Arabs had few names for flowers, the meaning is left to conjecture. It is also interesting that the color green is associated with both al-Khadir and the Buddha. "Al-Khadir" literally means "the Green Man," while the Buddha's lucky color is considered green, and he is often portrayed as green in statues.

Other remarkable similarities revolve around both lineage and location. A hadith mentioned by Ibn 'Ajībah in his commentary on the Qur'ān says:

> The Prophet ﷺ is reported to have said concerning al-Khadir, "He was the son of a king who desired that his son inherit his throne, but he refused and fled to a secluded island place where they could not find him."[20]

This is no different from the story of Gautama Buddha, a prince who fled his palace and sought out a secluded place in which to meditate. In a similar vein, Ibn 'Asākir also relates that al-Khadir ﷻ was a king's son who did not desire power or women, and he mentions that al-Khadir ﷻ remained celibate throughout his life.[21] Al-Alūsī, in his Qur'anic commentary, narrates that Abū Nu'aym, in his *Hilyah*, mentions that al-Khadir ﷻ was in India, as was the Buddha.

In addition, Ibn Kathīr (d. 1373) also relates two teachings of al-Khadir ﷻ that are surprisingly Buddhist in their essence. The first is on the authority of Wahab b. Munabbih (d. 729) who relates that

---

are other scholars who deny this and use as proof the well-known statement of the Prophet ﷺ that "within one hundred years, everyone on earth alive today will be dead." This hadith indicates, however, the meaning of *qarn* or "a generation," and does not negate the possibility of someone existing outside a normal lifespan. And God knows best.

19. 'Abd al-Razzāq, who relates the hadith said that "*al-farwat al-baydā*' which he sat upon was white herbage or its like, ... and others said it was a white plant that the Prophet ﷺ likened to white sheepskin." See Ibn Kathīr, *Qasas al-anbiyā'*, (Beirut: Tihāmah li al-Nashr wa al-Maktabāt, 1997), 349-351.

20. See Ahmad 'Ajībah, *al-Bahr al-madīd*, (18:65).

21. See Ibn Kathīr, *Qasas al-anbiyā'*, 454.

al-Khadir ﷺ said, "O Moses, people suffer in this world to the degree of their mental attachment to it."[22] According to the same book, when al-Khadir ﷺ departed from the company of Moses ﷺ, he left him with this advice: "Be beneficial wherever you go, and never cause any harm; be joyful and radiant, and do not become angry; leave disputation; never go anywhere without purpose; and never laugh without amazement."[23]

In the Qur'anic narrative, when al-Khadir ﷺ explains to Moses ﷺ the reasons why he committed the apparently inexplicable acts about which Moses ﷺ questions him, al-Khadir ﷺ gives as his reason, "It was all mercy from God that compelled me; I was not acting from my own concerns" (18:82). This exemplifies the Arahat's purpose in life. While discrepancy about the historical time period between that of Moses ﷺ and of the Buddha remains, the fact that Imam al-Shahrastānī could see the parallels between the teachings of the Buddha and of al-Khadir ﷺ stands as a powerful affirmation from a master Islamic theologian that, indeed, much of what we find in Buddhism is compatible with a Qur'anic worldview. One striking example is the Buddha's statement, "One who knows self is dear will keep it well guarded; the wise one keeps a vigil a third of the night."[24] Similarly, the Qur'ān states, "The Lord knows that you [Muhammad] keep vigil in the night, nigh two-thirds, or half the night, or a third" (73:20).

***

The history of Islam, not unlike the history of other religions, has its enlightened and its dark periods. In Islam's shared history with Buddhism, we find spans of time when Buddhists lived in relative peace and security under Muslim rule, and in other times, we find Muslims oppressing Buddhists, forcing them to convert or sometimes even massacring them. In some cases, we also find evidence of the Buddhist oppression of Muslims.

So it is worth looking back, not only at how well—or badly—Muslims and Buddhists have co-existed, but also at what the religion of Islam says about the Buddhists and their place in a Muslim dominated society.

---

22. This so accurately describes the basis of all Buddhist teaching that I will convey it in Arabic for those who wish to see that the translation is accurate. *Yā Mūsā, inna al-nāsa muʿadhabūna fī al-dunyā ʿalā qadri humūmihim bihā.* See Ibn Kathīr, *Qasas al-anbiyā'*, 352.

23. Ibid.

24. Cleary, 54.

Buddhism was widespread in Central Asia, Iran, Tibet, the Indian subcontinent, and China long before the Muslims arrived and interacted with them in these places. As Islam spread into Southeast Asia, Muslims encountered Buddhists in Burma, Cambodia, Vietnam, Siam and also the Malay archipelago. Buddhism thrived during the early period of the Muslim conquests, and historical accounts describe in great detail the temples and Buddhist schools in places such as Balkh and Mazaar-e-Sharif in today's northern Afghanistan. Moreover, sound records note the travels of the Chinese Buddhist monk and scholar, Hsuan Tsang, visiting Balkh around the year 630 and finding about one hundred Theravedic Buddhist monasteries there. The keepers of one of the most important shrines in Buddhist history were Persian–speaking Afghans, known as the Barmakids, who were brilliant Buddhist administrators. After their conversion to Islam, they were brought to Baghdad during the rule of the Abbasid dynasty, where they revolutionized Muslim government and introduced important diplomatic innovations that changed the face of Islam.

In the eighth century, when Qutaybah b. Muslim led the Umayyad Caliphate army into Central Asia, he found many people he described as idol worshippers, most of whom were probably Buddhists, but there were also Manichaeans and Nestorian Christians in these lands. According to Arab historians, Qutaybah was warned by the native people that anyone who harmed the statues would perish. However, he began to wipe them out, and upon seeing that he did not suffer or perish as a result, many of the superstitious embraced Islam.

Dr. Alexander Berzin, historian and scholar of Buddhism, writes about the early expansion of Islam into central Asia:

> [The Ummayyad governors] allowed followers of non-Muslim religions in the lands they conquered to keep their faiths if they submitted peacefully and paid a poll tax…. Although some Buddhists in Bactria and even an abbot of Nava Vihara converted to Islam, most Buddhists in the region accepted this *dhimmi* status as loyal non-Muslim protected subjects within the Islamic states. Nava Vihara remained open and functioning. The Han Chinese pilgrim Yijing (I-Ching) visited Nava Vihara in the 680s and reported it flourishing as a Sarvastivada center of study.

An Umayyad Arab author, al-Kermani, wrote a detailed account of Nava Vihara at the beginning of the eighth century, preserved in the tenth century work *Book of Lands* (Arabic: *Kitab al-Buldan*) by al-Hamadhani. He described it in terms readily understandable to Muslims by drawing the analogy with the Kaaba in Mecca, the holiest site of Islam. He explained that the main temple had a stone cube in the center, draped with cloth, and that devotees circumambulated it and made prostration, as is the case with the Kaaba. The stone cube referred to the platform on which a stupa stood, as was the custom in Bactrian temples. The cloth that draped it was in accordance with the Iranian custom for showing veneration, applied equally to Buddha statues as well as to stupas. Al-Kermani's description indicates an open and respectful attitude by the Umayyad Arabs in trying to understand the non-Muslim religions, such as Buddhism, that they encountered in their newly conquered territories.[25]

Nonetheless, opposition to Islam in these lands was violent, and non-Muslims were not allowed to carry weapons. Afghans maintain that Islam spread among them peacefully, but the historical record shows that Buddhism remained strong even after the Arab invasion up until the conversion of the king of Kabul during the reign of al-Ma'mūn (d. 833). A statue of the Buddha was sent to al-Ma'mūn as a tribute, and he had it shipped to Mecca where it remained on display for a few years, reminding all that the king of the Afghans had embraced Islam. This worked well as a bit of Abbasid propaganda in their efforts to spread Islam.

During the uprising of Imam al-Husayn in the Arabian peninsula, the Buddhists used the Ummayad neglect of Afghanistan as an opportunity to reclaim their sovereignty. In 705, the Tibetans allied with the Turki Shahis and attempted to drive the Ummayad forces from Bactria. In 708, the Buddhist prince, Nazaktar Khan, succeeded in removing the Ummayayd forces and "established a fanatic Buddhist rule in Bactria. He even beheaded the former abbot of Nava Vihara who had converted to Islam."[26]

Seven years later, the Arabs regained what was lost. The Mus-

25. Alexander Berzin, *Historical Sketch of Buddhism and Islam in Afghanistan*, 2006, (www.berzinarchives.com.), 5.

26. Ibid.

lim general, Qutaybah, recaptured Bactria from the Turki Shahis and their Tibetan allies. Qutaybah imposed harsh punishment on the monastery, which led to many Buddhist monks fleeing to Khotan and Kashmir, thus strengthening Buddhism in these areas. The temple was restored, and the general policy towards the Buddhists was toleration, unless they were involved in any subversive opposition to Muslim rule.[27]

The Tibetans, who had previously allied with the Turki Shahis, now allied with the Ummayyads and, in 717, sent an ambassador to the Ummayyad court of 'Umar b. 'Abd al-Azīz, who in turn sent a Muslim scholar, al-Hanafī, to Tibet to preach Islam to the Tibetans. He seems to have been unsuccessful. Buddhism remained strong in Central Asia for over a hundred years of Muslim rule, which indicates a general toleration of the religion.[28] But by the mid-ninth century, Islam began taking hold among the Central Asians, despite widespread practice of Buddhism. Thomas W. Arnold, a British orientalist and professor of Islamic Studies, writes:

> [The king of Kabul's] successors, however, seem to have relapsed to Buddhism, for when Ya'qūb b. Layth, the founder of the Saffārid dynasty, extended his conquests as far as Kābul in 871, he found the ruler of the land to be an "idolater," and Kābul now became really Muhammadan for the first time, the Afghans probably being quite willing to take service in the army of so redoubtable a conqueror as Ya'qūb b. Layth, but it was not until after the conquests of Sabaktigīn and Mahmūd of Ghazna that Islam became established throughout Afghanistan.[29]

The polymath scholar, al-Bayrūnī, acclaimed as the founder of comparative religious studies, noted the decline and gradual disappearance of Buddhism in Afghanistan after the tenth century. He described what was left of Buddhism in Afghanistan during his time and engaged both Hindus and Buddhists during his sojourn in India when he accompanied the invading Muslim army of Mahmoud al-Ghazni. Evidence suggests that Muslim architecture that was used to build madrasas was influenced by the architecture of Buddhist

---

27. Ibid., 4.
28. Ibid.
29. Thomas W. Arnold, *The Preaching of Islam* (New Delhi: Adam Publishers & Distributors, 2002), 217.

monasteries.[30] It is clear that up until the Mongol invasions of the thirteenth century, Buddhism was still widespread in Eastern Muslim lands, and Buddhists could be found in Iran and Central Asia.

After the Mongolian invasion of these lands, Muslims suffered greatly and many of their subjects found an opportunity to exact revenge for previous Muslim transgressions. The level of animosity felt against the Muslims by some of their previous subjects is illustrated in the following incident from the reign of Kuyūk Khan (1246-1248), the grandson of Genghis Khan, as recounted by the Muslim historian al-Jūzjānī:

> Trustworthy persons have related that Kuyūk was constantly being incited by the Buddhist priests to acts of oppression towards the [Muslims] and the persecution of the faithful. There was an Imām in that country, one of the men of learning among the Muslims ... named Nūr al-Dīn al-Khawārizmī. A number of Christian laymen and priests and a band of idol-worshipping Buddhist priests made a request to Kuyūk, asking him to summon that Imām of the [Muslims] that they might hold a controversy with him and get him to prove the superiority of the faith of Muhammad and his prophetic mission—otherwise, he should be put to death. The Khān agreed, the Imām was sent for, and a discussion ensued upon the claim of Muhammad to be a prophet and the manner of his life as compared with that of other prophets. At length, as the arguments of those accursed ones were weak and devoid of the force of truth, they withdrew their hand from contradiction and drew the mark of oppression and outrage on the pages of the business and asked Kuyūk Khān to tell the Imām to perform two genuflexions in prayer, according to the rites and ordinances of the [Muslim] law, in order that his unbecoming movements in the performance of this act of worship might become manifest to them and to the Khān.... When the godly Imām and the other [Muslim] who was with him had placed their foreheads on the ground in the act of prostration, some infidels whom Kuyūk had summoned, greatly annoyed them and knocked their heads with force upon the ground, and committed other abominable acts against them. But that godly Imām endured all this

---

30. Glasse, 302.

oppression and annoyance and performed all the required forms and ceremonies of the prayer and in no way curtailed it. When he had repeated the salutation, he lifted up his face towards heaven and observed the form of "invoke your Lord with humility and in secret," and having asked permission to depart, he returned unto his house.[31]

It is not surprising that Buddhists would have felt such hostility toward people that had so little regard for their faith and deemed them simply as "idolaters," no different than those under whom Muslims had suffered in Mecca during the early years of Islam.

Nevertheless, not all Buddhists during this period were antagonistic to Islam, and some had a real interest in the tenets of the faith. Among the most prominent converts to Islam from Buddhism was Ghāzan Khan, the seventh and greatest Ilkhānid ruler of the Mongol Empire. He was born a Christian, raised a Buddhist as a young boy, and went on to erect several Buddhist temples in Khorasan. He ruled in Persia and brought with him into that country several Buddhist priests who were kept in his court and with whom he enjoyed conversing. At the height of his power, after a thorough study of Islam, he seems to have had a genuine conversion experience. His chronicler, the noted Muslim historian Rashīd al-Dīn, defended the conversion as sincere and argued, "What interested motive could have led so powerful a sovereign to change his faith: much less, a prince whose pagan ancestors had conquered the world?"[32] Again, however, we find the Buddhists referred to as pagans.

***

There is no denying that we have this recurrent theme, both in the past and in the present, of Muslims labeling Buddhists as pagans, idolaters, or polytheists. This is somewhat compounded by the reality of the absolute disdain Muslims have for any forms of idolatry, even iconography. It is beyond the scope of this essay to adequately address the issue of whether Buddhism is an idolatrous form of worship. Suffice it to state that any such assertion would be a gross oversimplification, given the vast range of spiritual expression found under the umbrella of Buddhism. There are today Christian Buddhists, Jewish Buddhists, and Humanistic Buddhists, not to mention the variations found in history. The Bon influenced expressions of Cen-

---

31. Arnold, 225-226.
32. Ibid., 233.

tral Asia, for instance, are quite different from the Cha'n Buddhism of China or its Japanese expression in Zen. And Zen Buddhism certainly cannot be termed idolatrous, even by Islam's severe standards of idolatry.

Complicating matters for Muslim-Buddhist relations is the reality that many Muslims tend to conflate veneration with worship.[33] Despite Abū Hanīfah's acknowledgement that Sabians did not worship the stars but merely venerated them in the manner of Muslims venerating the Kaaba, Buddhist ritual and the widespread use of Buddha's image in their devotional practices continues to fuel the narrative of idol-worship, especially among those Muslims who bring a fundamentalist approach to their faith.

Furthermore, we must also acknowledge that most forms of Buddhism are described by Buddhists themselves as either agnostic or atheistic, which eliminates the problem of idolatry, but creates just as severe a problem for Muslims because it also eliminates the idea of God altogether. In this regard we should take particular note of one of the central contentions of Dr. Shah-Kazemi in this book: that those Buddhists who describe themselves as atheist are in fact going beyond anything the Buddha stated. For, as Shah-Kazemi notes, on p. 31 of this book: "Nobody can deny that the Buddha's doctrine is non-theistic: there is no Personal divinity playing the role of Creator, Revealer, Judge in Buddhism. But to assert that the Buddha's doctrine is 'atheistic' would be to attribute to him an explicit denial and negation of the Absolute—which one does not find anywhere in his teachings." In other words, Buddhists do have a concept of ultimate reality, which although not Abrahamic or personal, does correspond to God in a transpersonal sense. In the same vein, not unlike Islam, certain strains of Buddhism include belief in an afterlife, a form of heaven and hell, and places of joy and suffering. These are themes raised and discussed in this book in a manner which we hope will lead to fruitful dialogue between Muslims and Buddhists, rendering clearer both where we differ and where our "common ground" lies.

The fact that Muslims historically relegated Buddhism to idolatry is more a reflection of an ignorance of the depth of Buddhist teaching and less a reflection of an Islamic understanding of Buddhism. In many ways, Islam is a bridge between Asian truths found in the teachings of Buddhism, Taoism, Confucianism, and Vedantic

---

33. See in this connection the arguments of Shah-Kazemi upholding the non-idolatrous nature of Buddhist worship, pp. 58-78.

Hinduism and the truths found in the Abrahamic faiths of Judaism and Christianity.

Moreover, as has been clearly stated by Professor Kamali in his Foreword, and amplified by Dr. Shah-Kazemi, there were periods when Buddhists lived in safety under Muslim rule, paying a tribute (*jizyah*)[34] and were considered people of protected status (*dhimmah*), in accordance with the position of Imam Mālik (d. 795) and many Hanafī scholars, who permit protected status for non-Abrahamic religions, even ones which involve idolatry. Dr. Sādiq al-Ghiryānī explains this position:

> *Jizyah* is taken from the Arab idolaters and whoever practices a religion other than Islam among Christians, Jews, Magians, Communists, Hindus, and any others among worshipers of idols or fire given that the Prophet ﷺ himself commanded those going out in military expeditions to oppose enemies of Islam to first call them to Islam and "should they refuse then invite them to pay tribute," and he did not distinguish between a polytheist or the People of the Book, … and in the sound hadith recorded in Muslim on the authority of 'Abd al-Rahmān b. 'Awf ﷺ, the Prophet ﷺ took *jizyah* from the Magians of Hajar and Oman. Furthermore, on the authority of al-Zuhrī, Mālik states that the Prophet ﷺ took *jizyah* from the Magians of Bahrain, and 'Umar ﷺ accepted it from the Persians [and among them were Buddhists as well as the majority who were Zoroastrians], and 'Uthmān ﷺ accepted it from the Persians, and the Prophet ﷺ stated, "Treat them as you would the People of the Book."[35]

---

34. Though the word "tribute" is often viewed as unfavorable today, Webster's dictionary defines it as "a payment by one ruler or nation to another in acknowledgment of submission or as the price of protection." The *jizyah* is a formal tax paid by individuals living in a community under Muslim rule. Monastic orders are exempt from the tax, as are retired, disabled, and indigent people.

35. See Dr. Sādiq al-Ghiryānī, *al-Mudawwanah al-jadīdah* (Beirut: Mu'assasaat al-Rayyān, 2002), vol. 2, 454-59. He includes humanists and communists, which is consistent with Mālik's position but unfortunately is not known by many Muslims who mistakenly believe that this option was traditionally available only to Jews and Christians. However, this would not explain the status of Hindus in India under Muslim rule for the past several hundred years, despite unfortunate and un-Islamic periods of persecution.

Once people have entered into a protected status, irrespective of their religion, they are allowed to travel freely in the lands of Muslims; there is only one sacred area in the Arabian Peninsula that is exempted, as the Prophet ﷺ reserved it only for Muslims and asked his followers to relocate from that area those people who were practicing other religions, which included Jews, Christians, and polytheists. The mere fact that he mentioned the polytheists in this hadith is a clear indication that non-Muslims are not to be forced into conversion or killed if they refused conversion. A small minority of Muslim scholars, however, takes an extreme position, citing the Qur'anic verse which states that Muslims should seek out and kill those polytheists who violated their treaty with the Muslims by treacherously killing unarmed Muslims (9:5). Yet the verse immediately following that states, "But should they appeal to you for security, then grant them such in order for them to hear the word of God. And thereafter, escort them to a place where they can be secure. That is because they are people without knowledge" (9:6).

Even though Buddhists and Hindus were oppressed at times under Muslims, more often than not they were protected, as were their places of worship. Some also achieved positions of high rank in Muslim society. These were the times when Muslims were practicing the best of their tradition. The Prophet Muhammad ﷺ said, "Whoever oppresses a non-Muslim who has a covenant with Muslims, or who even belittles him or forces him to do something he is unable to do, or who takes from him anything that he is not satisfied in giving, I will argue against the Muslim on the Day of Judgment [on behalf of the non-Muslim.]"[36]

The age of tribute and protected status (*dhimmah*) of others under Muslim rule is long gone and only remains as a historical curiosity, notwithstanding its valid legal status as part of the shariah. The Prophet ﷺ predicted that the first aspect of the faith to be removed from the world would be governance. And once removed, he stated that it would remain so until the return of Jesus ﷺ, who would personally remove the tribute payment from the shariah. What matters today is that we build upon the positive precedents established by our tradition of tolerant jurisprudence, and encourage Muslims to consider Buddhists as being akin to "People of the Book." This is one of the main aims of the present initiative to seek *Common Ground* between Islam and Buddhism. There is an Islamic legal precedent

---

36. This is a sound hadith in Abū Dāwūd's collection, no. 2626.

for this in the hadith of the Prophet ﷺ in which we are told to treat the Magians as if they were People of the Book, with the exception of marrying their women and eating their meat.

***

Today, we live together in an increasingly interdependent world. The challenges facing us as a species behoove us to focus on our commonalities and our shared values. We are confronted with global crises of all types: environmental, economic, social, religious, and military, not to mention the tremendous natural disasters that are afflicting us on an increasingly frequent basis. Never before has human cooperation been needed so desperately, and never before has it been so imperative that we set aside our differences. Buddhism and Islam share profound precepts of charity, patience, forbearance, and a recognition that everything in the world is imbued with the sacred. We may speak of the sacred in different ways, using different words, but its essence is one. Buddhism teaches kindness, and Islam's essence is mercy, which is another word for kindness.

We often forget that kindness is engendered by a shared sense of "kind." "He is my kind of man," we say. When commonalities are accentuated and kindness is highlighted, we tend to treat others as our own kind, as related, as our "kin," a word that shares the same root with *gyn*, which means "womb" and is called *rahim* in Arabic, which relates to the word *rahmah*, meaning "mercy." The Qur'ān affirms all of humanity as being of one family: *Banu Adam*, humankind. When our common humanity and our kindred nature are brought to the forefront, kindness becomes not only possible but *natural*. Our earliest ancestors had valid reasons to fear strangers, but they also developed many traditions of honoring the familiar guest as well as the stranger. In the modern world, there is much to cause fear as well, but we must foster empathy, and cultivate and enhance our own ways of honoring the familiar guest and the stranger. While much evidence abounds to cause trepidation about succeeding at that task, I would argue that far more exists to inspire hope.

For the first time in human history, we have media at our fingertips enabling us to leap over vast stretches of land and sea instantaneously and communicate with people across the globe. From the comfort of our living rooms, we have the ability to see and understand how people of a different culture, ethnicity, or religion live their lives, and we are able to marvel at the richness and biodiversity of our planet. We delight in the diversity we find in nature; we are awed by the myriad varieties of flora and fauna; and we express our love with bouquets of varied and colorful flowers. Even the most curious strangers from distant lands are increasingly part of our collective consciousness.

Yet fear too often wells up when we are confronted with people who do not seem like us. We fall back on xenophobia, which literally means "a fear of the other." Oddly, it is often religion that causes divisiveness and dread when it ought to unite believers and inculcate in them the Golden Rule, which is a universal principle—thus at once sacred *and* secular--articulated by the Abrahamic prophets as well as the Asian sages from the Buddha to Confucius. Far too often, a distorted understanding of our faith traditions causes us to demonize the other as infidel or idolater, tyrant or terrorist, and as somehow less than human. While Buddhism seems to have less of this tendency than other faiths, it is not—and historically has not been—immune to these problems. Islam, which historically was more often than not a fount of tolerance in a xenophobic world, is now seen by some as being infected with intolerance. Sadly, some Buddhists are among those who have suffered at the hands of small numbers of misguided Muslims who attacked them and the temples of those they deemed to be "not of our kind."

Yet, if we look around the world today, there is much that we find heartening. Muslims live as minorities in Buddhist countries, such as Thailand and Tibet, and share neighborhoods in California with Buddhists. The Prophet ﷺ said, "Gentleness is never in a thing except that it embellishes it and is never removed from something except that it blemishes it."[37] Nothing in the Prophet's teaching allows mistreatment of others based upon their beliefs. Islam itself began under intense religious persecution, and the Prophet ﷺ was deeply sensitive to this fact and left teachings to ensure that Muslims did not fall victim to the very behaviors that victimized them.

While Buddhists also have their own history of violence,[38] today they are some of the gentlest and most peaceful people on earth.

---

37. Sahīh Muslim.

38. For a study in Japanese Buddhist use of violence see Mikael S. Adolphson's *The Teeth and Claws of the Buddha: Monastic Warriors and Sohei in Japanese History*. For an extraordinary study on religious violence during the last two thousand years, see Naveed S. Sheikh's *Body Count: A Quantitative Review of Political Violence Across World Civilizations*.

Their leaders often preach kindness and compassion throughout the world, and the Dalai Lama has publicly defended Muslims and their faith—at the Vatican and in other prominent venues—despite having been mistreated in his youth by some ignorant Tibetan Muslims.

It is time we recognize that many of the gravest and most vexing conflicts today are fueled by religious rhetoric that cloaks deeper causes, mostly greed, covetousness, and aggression, which are rooted in selfish and territorial interests. But it is true religion that can treat and remedy these very human ailments. Religion gets conscripted into such degrading battles by demagogues, and that in turn tragically alienates an increasingly large number of considerate and concerned people who begin to see religion as part of the problem. Until we address the very real calamities confronting our collective humanity with all the tools available to us—especially religion and a genuine concern for humanity and the myriad species that we share this marvelous world with—we are failing our faiths. It is undeniable that we come from different faiths and families, but we must also recognize that we are quintessentially of the larger human family.

It is our common humanity that binds us to one another and calls us to recognize all people as our kind. "We have dignified all of humankind," states the Qur'ān (17:70), while Buddhism reminds us that human suffering is caused by craving and selfish desire that must be countered by recognizing the impermanence of life and by inculcating compassion toward all sentient beings for the brief time we are here. Until we acknowledge our human nature, both the bestial and celestial sides, we are doomed to fail.

My own teacher, Shaykh Abdullah Bin Bayyah, once explained to me: "The dignity of humanity precedes the dignity of faith and is subordinate to it." In other words, a human is inviolable by virtue of his or her humanity, even before the inviolability of shared faith. The Prophet Muhammad ﷺ stated, "None of you truly believes until he loves for his fellow man what he loves for himself."[39] The great imams of Islam have argued that this mutual love and respect extends even to those who reject Islam, but can only be achieved by opposing one's selfish desires. Similarly, the Bodhisattva is devoted to the cause of releasing all of humanity from the chains of false desire.

Islam and Buddhism share so many virtuous qualities and concerns for humankind that when Muslims or Buddhists are unkind to

---

39. Imam al-Nawawī's Forty Hadith Collection, no. 13.

one another, it is no less than a failure of our leaders and teachers to help us understand our own traditions and our shared history. Increasing globalization demands that we affirm and accentuate the common bonds of universal kinship. If our faiths cannot facilitate this most important of tasks, then the professors, spiritual leaders, and claimants of such traditions have betrayed them by failing to live up to the sublime standards set by their respective prophets and founders.

***

In the best of times, Muslims have lived peacefully in many places with their Buddhist brethren. Buddhists lived under Muslim governance as protected people, and there is ample historical evidence to substantiate this. Their persons, properties, and temples were secure based upon the Qur'anic injunction, "God does not forbid you from being good to those who have not fought you" (60:8). The Qur'anic worldview is a pluralistic one that acknowledges the right of peoples to express their devotion in accordance with the dictates of their religion. It is clear that diversity is an expression of the divine itself, as the Qur'ān states, "Had God wanted, He would have made you all one people, but the intent is to test you, so vie with another in performing good works" (5:48).

The Prophet Muhammad ﷺ said about protected religious minorities living under Muslim rule, "Whoever hurts a non-Muslim citizen hurts me, and whoever hurts me has vexed God."[40] The great Hanafī jurist, Ibn 'Ābidīn (d. 1836), argued that since Muslims are responsible for protecting the life and property of non-Muslims, including the Buddhists, and since the persecution of the weak at the hands of the strong is among the greatest crimes in Islam, the persecution of non-Muslims, including the Buddhists, in an Islamic state is considered a greater crime than the persecution of Muslims by non-Muslims.[41]

Despite the Islamic jurists' recognition of Buddhism as being classified among the protected religions, some Muslims have difficulty accepting Buddhists and those of other Asian traditions as possibly being considered among the Sabians mentioned in the Qur'ān, and other Muslims simply consider the Buddhists idolatrous, given

---

40. Imam al-Bayhaqī, *al-Sunnan al-kubrā*, vol 5, 205. Narrated by al-Khatīb with an authentic chain.

41. 'Abd ar-Rahmān I. Doi, *Sharī'ah: Islamic Law*, revised and expanded by 'Abdassamad Clarke, (UK: Taha Publishers Ltd, 2008), 654.

their veneration of the images of the Buddha and its association with idolatry. For all such Muslims today, I would like to narrate a story from the Islamic tradition, once related by the sages of Islam to teach how to treat others, no matter what their beliefs are. Imam Sīdī al-Mukhtār al-Kuntī al-Shingittī relates in his book *Fath al-Wadūd* the following:

> It is related that an idolater once sought refuge with Abraham 鴾 and asked for nourishment. Upon seeing an idolater, Abraham 鴾 refused him and sent him off. Angel Gabriel 鴾 appeared and said to Abraham 鴾, "I bring the greeting of peace from your Lord, who asks you, 'Why did you turn away My servant?'"
>
> Abraham 鴾 replies, "Because he was an idolater."
>
> "God asks you, 'Did you create him or did I?'"
>
> Abraham 鴾 replies, "Of course, You created him."
>
> "God asks you, 'Was his disbelief in Me or in you?'"
>
> Abraham 鴾 responds, "His disbelief was in You."
>
> "God asks you, 'Were you providing for him all these years or was I?'"
>
> Abraham 鴾 replies, "Indeed, You are my provider as well as his."
>
> "God asks, 'Did He create that disbelief in his heart, or did you create it and nurture it in him?'"
>
> Abraham 鴾 says, "No, You did."
>
> "God asks you whether his disbelief harmed him or you?"
>
> Abraham 鴾 replies, "No, it harmed him."
>
> "God says, 'If that is the case, then why did you deprive My servant and your brother? For he is in one of two possible conditions: fuel for the fire and an object of My wrath, or I can forgive him and make him among my beloveds and grant him peace in the abode of My mercy.'"
>
> At this point, Abraham 鴾 went out in search of the man and found he was now fearful of him. He showed the man kindness and cajoled him into returning to his tent to feed him. The man said, "Something happened, as you are acting so differently towards me. Initially you refused me, and now you are showing me kindness, as if you want something from me."

Abraham ﷺ said to him, "My Lord reproached me for the way I treated you."

To this the man said, "What a blessed Lord you have that He should reproach His beloved due to his bad behavior toward His enemy." He then submitted to the God of Abraham ﷺ and worshipped with him until he died.[42]

This story—not necessarily its ending—illustrates the essential aim of both the *A Common Word* initiative and the present *Common Ground* project: inviting into our tent the stranger who may not look, worship, or be like us in many ways, *because* he or she is a creation of God, here for a purpose, and someone to be honored as a fellow guest of God. We are committed to setting an example and embodying in our attitudes, declarations, and behaviors the very change we wish to see manifest in the world. The challenge before us is to understand our teachings better—from within and without—so we can engender a true celebration of humankind's diversity. For indeed, too many of us seem to have just enough faith to foment hatred, oppression, and fear among people, but not nearly enough to nurture kindness, compassion, and mercy.

---

42. Imam Sīdī al-Mukhtār al-Kuntī al-Shingittī, *Fath al-Wadūd* (Damascus: Matbaʿat al-Kitāb al-ʿArabiy, 1991), 325.

Biographies of Contributors

Dr. Reza Shah-Kazemi is the author of works in the field of Islamic studies and comparative religion, including:

My Mercy Encompasses All—The Koran's Teachings on Compassion, Peace and Love (Emeryville, CA: Shoemaker and Hoard, 2007)
Paths to Transcendence—According to Shankara, Ibn Arabi and Meister Eckhart (Bloomington, IN: World Wisdom Books, 2006)
Justice and Remembrance: Introducing the Spirituality of Imam Ali (London: IB Tauris, 2006)
The Other in the Light of the One: The Universality of the Qur'an and Interfaith Dialogue (Cambridge: Islamic Texts Society, 2006).

He is currently managing editor of *Encyclopaedia Islamica* at the Institute of Ismaili Studies, London, a Fellow of the Royal Aal al-Bayt Institute of Islamic Thought in Amman, and serves on the advisory boards of several journals in the field of comparative religion.

* * *

H. R. H. Prince Ghazi bin Muhammad bin Talal (b. 1966) is the first cousin of H. M. King Abdullah II of Jordan, and the nephew of the late H. M. King Hussein. He attended Harrow School (UK); received a BA *Summa Cum Laude* from Princeton University; received his first PhD from Cambridge University, UK in 1993 and his second from Al-Azhar University, Cairo, in 2010. He has held numerous high posts in Jordan, and is currently Personal Envoy and Special Advisor to H. M. King Abdullah. He founded the *National Park for the Site of the Baptism of Jesus Christ* (1996); *Al-Belqa University* in Jordan (1996); *Altafsir.com* (the largest on-line Quranic resource (2001); and the *World Islamic Sciences and Education University* (2007). He is also (part-time) Professor of Philosophy at Jordan University. He holds a number of high decorations and awards, and has published a number of books. He was the author of the historic *A Common Word* Open Letter and Peace Initiative of 2007.

* * *

Professor Mohammad Hashim Kamali is Founding Chairman and CEO of the International Institute of Advanced Islamic Studies, Malaysia (2007–), and a world renowned scholar in Islamic jurisprudence. He served as Professor of Islamic Law and Jurisprudence at the International Islamic University Malaysia (IIUM, 1985–2004); and was Dean of the International Institute of Islamic Thought and Civilisation (ISTAC, 2004–2006). Currently he is Senior Fellow at the Institute of Strategic and International Studies (ISIS) Malaysia, a Senior Fellow of the Academy of Sciences of Afghanistan, and also Senior Fellow of the Royal Academy of Jordan. He serves on the International Advisory Board of thirteen academic journals published in Malaysia, the United States, Canada, Kuwait, India, Australia and Pakistan. Professor Kamali has served as a member and sometime Chairman of the Constitution Review Commission of Afghanistan (2003); as a United Nations consultant on constitutional reforms in Afghanistan, the Maldives, and Iraq; and currently advises the United Nations on a new constitution for Somalia. His books *Principles of Islamic Jurisprudence, Freedom of Expression in Islam, A Textbook of Hadith Studies*, and *Shari'ah Law: An Introduction* are standard text books in English speaking universities worldwide.

* * *

Shaykh Hamza Yusuf was born in Walla Walla, Washington, and adopted Islam at the age of eighteen. Subsequently, he migrated to the Middle East, where he spent more than ten years studying Islamic sciences on the Arabian Peninsula and in North and West Africa. He returned to the United States and during the last twenty years has been teaching and writing in the U.S. He is the author of *Purification of the Heart* and has translated into modern English several classical Arabic texts and poems, including *The Burda: The Poem of the Cloak* and *The Creed of Imam al-Tahawi*. Through his numerous lectures and media appearances, he has been active in the ongoing public discourse about Islam, nationally and internationally. He currently is involved in establishing Zaytuna College, the first accredited Muslim college in America. He resides in Northern California with his wife and five boys.

138

Bibliography

Aronson, Harvey. *Love and Sympathy in Theravada Buddhism.* Delhi: Motilal Banarsidass, 1980.

Arnold, Thomas W. *The Preaching of Islam.* New Delhi: Adam Publishers & Distributors, 2002.

Badawi, Mostafa. 'The Muhammadan Attributes'. *Seasons— Semiannual Journal of Zaytuna Institute*, vol. 2, no.2 (Spring-Summer 2005).

al-Balādhurī, Abū al-Hasan. *Futūh al-buldān.* Beirut: Maktaba al-Hilāl, 1988.

al-Bukhārī, *Sahīh.* Translated by M.M. Khan. Riyadh: Makataba Dar-us-Salam, 1994.

Cleary, Thomas, trans. *Dhammapada: The Sayings of Buddha.* New York: Bantam Books, 1994.

———. *The Flower Ornament Scripture—A Translation of the Avatamsaka Sutra.* Boulder & London: Shambhala, 1984.

Coomaraswamy, Ananda. *Buddha and the Gospel of Buddhism.* New Jersey: Citadel Press, 1988.

Conze, Edward. *Buddhism—A Short History.* Oxford: Oneworld, 2000.

———. *Buddhist Scriptures.* Baltimore, 1968.

———. *Buddhist Wisdom Books.* London: George Allen & Unwin, 1958.

Conze, E., & I.B. Horner, D. Snelgrove, A. Waley, eds. *Buddhist Texts Through the Ages.* Oxford: Bruno Cassirer, 1954.

Doi, 'Abd al-Rahmān I. *Sharī'ah: Islamic Law* (revised and expanded by 'Abdassamad Clarke). London: Taha Publishers, 2008.

Evans-Wentz, W.Y. *Tibet's Great Yogī Milarepa.* London: Humphrey Milford, 1928.

Friedmann, Yohanan. *Tolerance and Coercion in Islam—Interfaith Relations in the Muslim Tradition.* Cambridge: Cambridge University Press, 2003.

Fu'ād, Anwar, Abū Khuzām, *Mustalahāt al-Sūfiyyah.* Beirut: Maktabat Lubnan, 1993.

al-Ghazzali, Abū Hāmid. *The Book of Knowledge.* Translated by Nabih Amin Faris. Lahore: Sh. Muhammad Ashraf, 1970.

————. *Al-Ghazālī: Invocations and Supplications* (Book IX of *Ihyā' 'ulūm al-dīn*). Translated and edited by K. Nakamura. Cambridge: Islamic Texts Society, 1990.

————. *Al-Ghazālī—The Niche of Lights*. Translated by David Buchman. Provo, Utah: Brigham Young University Press, 1998.

————. *Al-Ghazālī—The Remembrance of Death and the Afterlife*. Translated and edited by T.J. Winter. Cambridge: Islamic Texts Society, 1989.

————. *Ihyā' 'ulūm al-dīn*. Beirut: Dār al-Jīl, 1992.

————. *Kitāb al-Arba'īn fī usūl al-dīn*. Beirut: Dar al-Afaq al-Abadiyya, 1979.

————. *Majmū'āt rasā'il al-Ghazzālī*. Beirut: Dār al-Kutub al-'Ilmiyyah, 1994.

al-Ghiryānī, Sādiq. *al-Mudawwanah al-jadīdah*. Beirut: Mu'assasaat al-Rayyān, 2002.

Glasse, Cyril. *The New Encyclopedia of Islam*. Walnut Creek, CA: AltaMira Press, 2003.

Hanh, Thich Nhat. *The Heart of the Buddha's Teaching*. Berkeley: Parallax Press, 1988.

Harris, Elizabeth J. *Detachment and Compassion in Early Buddhism*. Kandy, Sri Lanka: Buddhist Publication Society, 1997.

His Holiness, the Dalai Lama, 'Harmony, Dialogue and Meditation', in D.W. Mitchell & J.Wiseman, eds. *The Gethsemani Encounter*. New York: Continuum, 1999.

————. *The Good Heart: A Buddhist Perspective on the Teachings of Jesus*. Somerville: Wisdom Publications, 1996.

————. *The Many Ways to Nirvana*. London: Hodder and Stoughton, 2004.

————. *Widening the Circle of Love*. Translated by Jeffrey Hopkins. London & Sydney: Rider, 2002.

Ibn Kathīr, Ismā'īl. *Qasas al-anbiyā'*. Beirut: Tihamah li al-Nashr wa al-Maktabāt, 1997.

Ibn Nadīm, Abū al-Faraj Muhammad. *Al-Fihrist*. Beirut: Dār al-Ma'rifah, n.d.

Ibn Taymiyyah, Taqī al-Dīn Ahmad. *Al-Mawsū'ah al-muyassarah*. Riyad, n.d.

Ibrahim, E., & D. Johnson-Davies (trs.). *Forty Hadith Qudsi*. Beirut: Dar al-Koran al-Kareem, 1980.

Ikram, S.M. *History of Muslim Civilization in India and Pakistan*. Lahore: Institute of Islamic Culture, 1989.

al-Isfahānī, al-Rāghib, *Mu'jam mufradāt alfāz al-Qur'ān*. Beirut: Dār al-Fikr, n.d.

al-Iskandarī, Ibn 'Atā'Allāh. *The Key to Salvation—A Sufi Manual of Invocation*. Translated by Mary Ann Koury Danner. Cambridge: Islamic Texts Society, 1996.

Iyad, Qadi. *Ash-Shifā'*. Translated by Aisha Abdarrahman Bewley as *Muhammad—Messenger of Allah*. Inverness: Madinah Press, 1991.

Jabre, Farid. *La Notion de la Ma'rifa chez Ghazālī*. Paris: Traditions les Lettres Orientales, 1958.

Jamme, Albert. 'Inscriptions on the Sabaean Bronze Horse of the Dumbarton Oaks Collection', in *Dumbarton Oaks Papers*, vol. 8 (1954).

Jayatilleke, K.N. *Early Buddhist Theory of Knowledge*. London: George Allen & Unwin, 1963.

Kalupahana, David J. *Nāgārjūna—The Philosophy of the Middle Way*. New York: State University of New York Press, 1986.

Kanamatsu, Kenryo. *Naturalness—A Classic of Shin Buddhism*. Bloomington: World Wisdom, 2002.

Khushalani, Gobind. *Chachnamah Retold—An Account of the Arab Conquest of Sindh*. New Delhi: Promilla, 2006.

Lings, Martin. *The Holy Qur'ān—Translations of Selected Verses*. Cambridge: Royal Aal al-Bayt Institute & The Islamic Texts Society, 2007.

Mascaró, Juan (tr.). *The Dhammapada—The Path of Perfection*. Penguin: Harmondsworth, 1983.

Milarepa. *The Hundred Thousand Songs of Milarepa*. Translated by Garma C.C. Chang. Shambhala: Boston & Shaftsbury, 1989.

Mukhkh al-'ibāda. Beirut: Dār al-Hāwī, 2008.

Nanamoli, Bhikku, & Bikku Bodhi (trs.). *The Middle Length Discourses of the Buddha—A Translation of the Majjhima Nikāya*. Oxford: The Pali Texts Society, 1995.

Ormsby, Eric. *Ghazali—The Revival of Islam*. Oxford: Oneworld, 2008.

Pachow, W. *Chinese Buddhism—Aspects of Interaction and Reinterpretation*. Lanham MD: University Press of America, 1980.

Pallis, Marco. *A Buddhist Spectrum*. London: George Allen & Unwin, 1980.

———. *The Way and the Mountain*. London: Peter Owen, 1991.

Price, A.F., & Mou-Lam Wong (trs.). *The Diamond Sutra and The Sutra of Hui-Neng*. Boston: Shambhala, 1990.

Ray, Reginald. *Secret of the Vajra World*. Boston and London: Shambhala, 2002.

Red Pine (tr). *The Zen Teaching of Bodhidharma*. New York: North Point Press, 1987.

Rustom, M. 'Psychology, eschatology, and imagination in Mulla Sadra Shirazi's commentary on the hadith of awakening'. *Islam and Science*, vol.5, no.1 (1997).

Schimmel, Annemarie. *And Muhammad is His Messenger—The Veneration of the Prophet in Islamic Piety*. Chapel Hill and London: University of North Carolina Press, 1985.

Shah-Kazemi, Reza. 'God "The Loving"', in Miroslav Volf, Ghazi bin Muhammad, Melissa Yarrington (eds.). *A Common Word—Muslims and Christians on Loving God and Neighbor*. Grand Rapids, Michigan/Cambridge UK: William B. Eerdmans, 2010.

———. *The Other in the Light of the One—The Holy Qur'ān and Interfaith Dialogue*. Cambridge: Islamic Texts Society, 2006.

al-Shahrastānī, Muhammad b. 'Abd al-Karīm. *Kitābal-milal wa al-nihal*. Beirut: Dār al-Kutub al-'Ilmiyyah, n.d.

Shemesh, A. Ben. 'Some Suggestions to Qur'an Translators'. *Arabica*, vol.16, no.1, (1969).

Sheng-yen, Master. *Complete Enlightenment*, part 9, volume 7. New York: Dharma Drum, 1997.

al-Shingittī, al-Mukhtār al-Kuntī. *Fath al-Wadūd*. Damascus: Matba'at al-Kitāb al-'Arabī, 1991.

Shunjo. *Honen, The Buddhist Saint: His Life and Teaching*. Translated by H.H. Coates, & R. Ishizuka. New York: Garland, 1981.

Soonthorndhammathada, Phra. *Compassion in Buddhism and Purānas*. Delhi: Nag Publishers, 1995.

al-Suyūtī, Jalāl al-Dīn. *Al-Jāmi' al-Saghīr*. Beirut: Dar al-Ma'rifa, 1972.

Suzuki, D.T. 'The Buddhist Conception of Reality', in Frederick Franck, ed., *The Buddhist Eye*. Bloomington: World Wisdom, 2004.

———. *Essays in Zen Buddhism*. London: Rider & Company, 1970.

———. *On Indian Mahayana Buddhism*. New York: Harper & Row, 1968.

Trungpa, Chogyam. *Cutting Through Spiritual Materialism*. Boston: Shambhala, 1973.

Walser, Joseph. *Nāgārjūna in Context*. New York: Columbia University Press, 2005.

Wang, Youru. *Linguistic Strategies in Daoist Zhuangzi and Chan Buddhism*. London & New York: RoutledgeCurzon, 2003.

Watt, W. Montgomery. *The Faith and Practice of Al-Ghazali*. London: George Allen & Unwin, 1953.

Woodward, F.L. (tr.). *Some Sayings of the Buddha According to the Pali Canon*. London: Oxford University Press, 1925.

Yusuf, Hamza. *The Burda of al-Busiri*. Thaxted: Sandala, 2002.

———. "Who are the Disbelievers?" *Seasons—Semiannual Journal of Zaytuna Institute*, vol. 5, no. 1 (2008).